The Mime Book

The Mime Book

BY CLAUDE KIPNIS

Edited and Coordinated by Neil Kleinman

Photographs by Edith Chustka

An Umbrella Book

HARPER & ROW, PUBLISHERS

New York, Evanston, San Francisco, London

THE MIME BOOK. Copyright © 1974 by Claude Kipnis. All rights reserved. Printed in the United States of America. No part of this book may be used or reproduced in any manner whatsoever without written permission except in the case of brief quotations embodied in critical articles and reviews. For information address Harper & Row, Publishers, Inc., 10 East 53rd Street, New York, N.Y. 10022. Published simultaneously in Canada by Fitzhenry & Whiteside Limited, Toronto.

FIRST EDITION

Designed by Janice Stern, Neil Kleinman, Edith Chustka

LIBRARY OF CONGRESS CATALOGING IN PUBLICATION DATA

Kipnis, Claude.
  The mime book.

  (An Umbrella book)
  1. Mime.   I. Title.
PN2071.G4K5   792.3   73-14266
ISBN 0-06-012404-0

Contents

Exercises

Preface

This book is the result of a joint enterprise. Neil Kleinman and I met in 1968, while we were both at the University of Illinois, Urbana. I was an artist in residence; he was on the faculty and was co-editor of Depot Press, an experimental press that grew out of Depot, Inc., a center for performing and creative arts. After one of my public lecture-demonstrations, he approached me with an idea: a Mime flip-book that would put my conceptions and teachings about Mime in the form of a book. It turned out that we could not do the book then, but neither of us forgot the idea; two years later, we returned to the project. He had just started a publishing group, Umbrella Press/Publications, Inc. I had been on tour, taking time every now and then to scribble notes toward a possible book.

This book is the beneficiary of Umbrella's energy and imagination. It found the publisher; it prepared the book for publication, editing it, coordinating the material and its production, as well as working on its design and layout.

Neil Kleinman has been more than an editor and coordinator. He helped me frame and assemble most of the material in the windows, and he suggested and made changes in both the style and the structure of the manuscript. In a real sense, he served as my translator, since many of my words and thoughts (not to mention my pantomime!) were, to begin with, in French. All of this participation was crucial in making possible the transition from the forum of teaching and lecturing to the form of a book.

Claude Kipnis
December 1973

The Mime Book

Introduction

There are two kinds of books one can write about a subject like Mime. The first treats Mime as an art, which of course it is, and talks about it primarily from a theoretical and aesthetic point of view. The second kind takes a more functional approach. How does one do it? What exactly does one do when one is doing Mime? I was tempted to write about the art of Mime, not only because of the grandeur of the theme but also because of the fact that it is difficult to understand *how* to do something if one does not know *why* to do it.

Despite this temptation, I chose to write a more functional book, one specifically concerned with the mechanisms and techniques of Mime. I found that too few books were interested in the individual student trying to perform individual exercises. For this reason, I have made the practical central to this book.

Professional debts are hard to define and certainly hard to repay. None of us springs full-grown out of the head of Zeus; yet each of us is in debt to personal experiences and the acci-dents of experiences. For my part, I owe much to Etienne De-croux, whose book *Paroles sur le Mime* I admire profoundly; and I owe much to Marcel Marceau, under whose direction I spent a few enlightening months. Still, much that I know and much that is in this book was shaped by years of my own work in Mime on and off stage. For that reason, I think it is fair to warn the reader that the approach toward Mime taken in this book—both its organization and its content—is idiosyncratic; other mimes may not always agree, or agree only in part, with what I have to say. Disagreement about Mime is not in fact bad; it will help enlarge the art and enrich our skills.

Mime is a craft, and, like all crafts, it has bits and pieces of technique and skills that must be mastered before one can appreci-ate them. Nevertheless, I have not forgotten that Mime is also an art, and therefore I do not skimp on theory. But, for me, theories always percolate more naturally out of the action one performs.

I hold an imaginary glass in my hand, and it becomes visible, both to me and to my audience. The imaginary made visible, made tangible, is the very begin-ning of what Mime is; it is also at the beginning of aesthetic awareness. For this reason, the reader will not lack for theory, but it will be theory that springs from specific exercises in a con-crete space.

Since Mime is visual and ex-ists in a three-dimensional world, this book tries to be both visual and three-dimensional. It is only an illusion, of course, for how can one really make a linear world three-dimensional? (For that matter, how can one use words to show what silence is like?) In order to put a book on Mime into time and space, it is constructed as a flip-book, so that as you flip its pages, you will see a series of exercises per-formed. Flip it slowly and you will see the story unravel in one way; flip it faster and you will see the story unravel in another. You may stop and concentrate on one moment of the exercise frozen in time, like the jester in

the Tarot deck poised above the abyss; *or* you may flip through completely and see that the exercise has a beginning, middle, and end. Your timing will determine what it is you see, what it is you understand.

TOWARD A WORKING CONTEXT. I think we all have witnessed some form of Mime somewhere or other. From the declared pantomime performance to the less conscious mimicry of daily conversations, the range of experience is wide; yet perhaps some basic observations can cover it. We have all used such expressions as "He talks with his hands!" or "Imagine! Without a word!" or "It looked real!" All point to the fact that miming is a non-verbal activity that has something in common with language (it can almost be understood in the same way that words are understood). Mime seems to be a way of expressing oneself and, in particular, a way of expressing "things" and "situations" with the use of only the body.

Let us try out the following definition: *Mime is the art of re-*

Re-creating the World

Re-creating the world is a quick yet comprehensive way to say that Mime transposes reality from one mode to another. Mime cannot create a reality; it is a part of reality. Mime can only create a shape, a focus, for a substance that already exists. The water poured from a vase into a flat pan does not change; the quality and amount are the same. Mime provides a new mold for what we already know.

Putting aside the question of reality for the moment, let us look at the way Mime permits us to see how a world is made over again. Yesterday I ate an apple, and today I eat one. Tomorrow I shall eat one too. I *repeat* the act, but I do not re-create it. But if I should see all of these moments of eating an apple as *the* same moment, and all apples as *the* same apple, I come close to re-creating the act of eating an apple. The Mime world is a world in which acts can be re-created; it is a world in which the mime presents universal acts, over and over again, without end and yet without repetition. The apple is always being eaten for the first time and, for that matter, the last time too.

I hope we can agree that "reality" is a plastic term. It includes the "prosaic" and the "dream." The fact that nothing is changed by Mime does not mean that our apprehension of the world remains the same. Mime, in fact, lets us see the old in a new way. Take, for example, Marcel Marceau's pantomime "Birth, Youth, Maturity, Old Age, and Death." There is nothing more "real" than his rendition of this life cycle. Yet it all takes place in one minute. Its condensation of time makes it both unreal and real. Marceau has enabled us to see the form of life, something we could not hope to see so completely in real life, where so much time elapses from the beginning to the end that we forget what we have already seen and what we already know.

creating the world by moving and positioning the human body. As definitions go, this may sound a little ambitious, but it does have the advantage of being inclusive. Unfortunately, a bit too inclusive. The same definition might be used for other forms of art. For example, it would be true for sculpture when it uses the human form, and it would certainly be true for dance. It is necessary, then, to restrict this definition a bit, and we can do so by adding a crucial factor: the illusion of reality.

The mime "makes believe." Left to himself, with nothing and nobody around him, the mime acts in such a way that his audience not only understands but actually "sees" the world of objects and beings created before him. Then: *Mime is the art of creating the illusion of reality.*

This definition is still a little too ample and calls for some filling in. The mime re-creates the world around him as well as re-presenting and expressing his own inner world for others to see. The "outer" world contains objects, people, animals, organic life of all sorts, the sum and substance of his environment. The "inner" world consists of his own feelings, his thoughts, his impulses, his dreams. The mime must make an outer world seem to exist; at the same time, he must express his inner world of imagination. The art of Mime begins where and when these two worlds meet.

For instance: I imagine an apple. For me it is real, but, at the moment, only for me. I look at this apple, a look that establishes my desire and creates the image of something out there beyond me. You who watch cannot see it yet, but it begins to exist. There is now a fixed point in space, a vanishing point that should lead somewhere from something. In time, I will grab the apple, then bite into it. Now you will see the apple, my apple, completely. Now Mime is present. The two worlds of inner and outer space have met.

We are at the beginning of an open cycle where objects and feelings interact, defined by the action. In turn, what has just been created redefines the mime

5

himself, who reacts to what he now sees. And so it goes. Meanings, actions, and identities evolve in the space between the actor and the acted upon, the grabber and the grabbed, between the real and the imaginary.

In this process of creation, the mime has nothing but his body. And this body must make visible and understandable an imaginary world. With this, we become conscious of another level of the mime's performance. We have already seen the interaction between the inner and outer worlds; but now we see another interaction, between the performance itself and the spectators—those whom the mime hopes to make see and understand. The mime remains witless unless there is a spectator who can see the invisible as well as the visible which is being offered.

Clearly, this spectator also

The Spectator and the Performance

At the performance of a written piece, the sensibility of each spectator is jolted in direct proportion to his disposition, greater or lesser, to be moved. For this reason, from the least sensitive spectator to the most sensitive, there is a world of nuances, a shade of perception specific to each spectator. Because of this, something seems quite obvious to me: it is that the expression of the dialogue used by the author must be either above or below the level of the sensibilities of the majority of the spectators. The cold man, little prone to emotion, must almost always find it exaggerated and even gigantic; while the emotional spectator who is easily excited must often find it weak and slow. From this I conclude that the expressions of the poet are rarely at one with the sensibility of the spectator, unless one supposes that the charm of diction puts all the spectators at the same level—a proposition I find hard to accept.

Pantomime does not seem to me to have this inconvenience. It indicates the situation and the sentiments of each character only by steps, gestures, movements, and by the expression of the physiognomy; and it leaves each spectator with the task of adding his own dialogue, which is all the more just because it is always in terms of the emotion received.

Jean Georges Noverre,
Lettres sur les Arts Imitateurs
(Paris, 1807)

must have the power of imagination, if he is to see what is not there. When we praise the performer's imagination, we must not forget his debt to the spectator's imagination. It is the spectator who does the imagining. He must relate movements he sees to things he knows; he must keep track of an invisible environment, one sometimes in motion. He must provide words where there are no words and substance when there is only air. Recognizing this very special relation between the mime and his audience, I should like to add a bit more to my working definition of Mime: *Mime is the art of imagining the world together with others.*

However we define Mime, we may at least conclude that the mime must "catch" the spectator's attention and "tame" his imagination. To do so, the mime has to master the void and re-place the "invisible" by the "imaginary." For such a task, the mime has only his body. It is his tool; and as with any tool, the user must learn its potential and learn how to control it.

With something of a Cartesian spirit, in this book I "analyze" the body, first dividing it into functional segments in order to study the workings of each one separately. Later I "synthesize" the parts in order to demonstrate how they work together. I hope by this method to show how to improve control over each part of the body and to show how to develop the potential of the entire body to move and express itself. At times we shall even discover unsuspected possibilities— for example, "listening with the neck." Above all, I shall show how to use our bodies "efficiently" so that we can know what each part is able to do and can make it perform on demand.

Part One: The Body

1. Isolation

In order to isolate the various parts of the body, we must find a position from which to operate, one that signifies nothing in itself. As a neutral position, it should "say" nothing, either about our physical or our psychological attitude. Let us call this reference point Position Zero. It consists of standing perfectly *straight* and *immobile*. By *straight,* I mean that each part of the body rests, well centered, on the part which supports it. By *immobile,* I mean that the body is motionless. We shall choose among the many possible positions of the feet the one that provides the best base for our balance: an equilateral triangle.

Holding Position Zero is itself quite a task, but assuming that we can now stand straight and motionless, the next step is to move *one* element of the body without moving *any* other part. In other words, we are going to isolate one part from the rest of the body. This may sound simple and easy. It is simple, but not easy. The body is not used to staying still.

The difficulty in the isolation

11

exercises resides in the basic continuity between the moving part and the rest of the body; when one part moves, the parts that surround it naturally wish to move. In fact, it is relatively easy to move most segments of the body; we shall find that it is more difficult *not* to move. As a measure of success in these exercises, look carefully at what you are *not* moving. How well can you keep your body immobile while moving only one part?

To begin with, it will be hard to maintain the immobility of the rest of the body. One should start the exercises outlined in this book by doing them very slowly, progressively accelerating as immobility of the body is secured. Since these exercises are a form of gymnastics, it is worth taking time to warm up the muscles and loosen the joints in order to avoid needless strain and pain.

12

The Head

The Extremities

The extremities of the body are the hands, the feet, and the head. It is with extremities that we establish contact with the environment. Through them we register our relationship to the outside world and know that we have been "touched" by something or someone. In the world of the mime, incidentally, there is often little difference between touching and being touched. It is true, for instance, that we touch the wall; we don't normally say that the wall has touched us. But the mime must feel the wall touching him. The inanimate is alive, reaching out to become real. The mime reverses the normal pattern in another way. Words come to us as we listen; we can afford to be passive. The mime tilts his head, "cocks" his ears, "uses" his ears in order to listen. For the mime, there is only a thin line between actions and reactions, between what we know to be there and what we want to imagine.

In the pictures on page 111 and the flip sequence which begins on page 210, you can see how the extremities are moved to create the effect of physical reactions. What is most important in these sequences is that you can see the space which surrounds the mime, the objects and events which caused his reactions. In one you can see a man "pulled" and jerked by a rope. You can see the rope; more curious even, you can imagine another man, the man at the other end of the rope—his motions and perhaps a bit of his motives . . . whether he is mad, or playful, or coy.

There is no need to emphasize the importance of the head. We have come to believe that all emotions and feelings radiate out from it. Certainly the head and its brain have come to symbolize intelligence and authority—and power itself. But while the head is important, we should be careful not to exaggerate its significance, especially when we think in terms of performance. I shall want to recall this later when we consider the trunk and chest because the mime is careful to distribute many emotions to other parts of the body. For now, though, we should agree that the head can be considered to be sovereign, but only as it represents the mind: the sixth sense.

It is worth remembering that of all our extremities, the head is often the most exposed. We can hide our hands—put them in our pockets or put them be-

13

hind our back. We can curl up so our feet don't show. We can drape ourselves so that no one can see any part of our body. But it is difficult to make our head disappear.

It is important to know that the head has motions and expressions of its own. We can begin to understand the nature of these motions by combining them with other movements. When the head works "with" or "against" other parts of the body, meaning is greatly multiplied and the range of expressions is greatly expanded.

To learn how to move the head without moving other parts of the body, perhaps it will help if we understand how the head moves. It rests on the equivalent

Head working against the face.

Head working with the face.

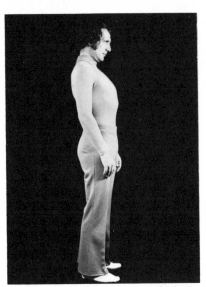

Head working against the body.

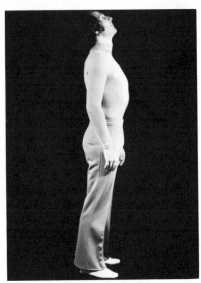

Head working with the body.

14

Yes! No!

In the set of exercises for the head, I will explain how to do the exercises by asking you, in one case, to nod your head as though you were saying "yes" and, in another, to shake it as though you were saying "no." But it is worth remembering that there is rarely a direct relationship between a Mime movement and the verbal meaning of our daily gestures. It happens that an up-down motion is for most of us the same thing as a nod in agreement—but this is nothing more than a convenient accident. (In India, for instance, my presentation of these exercises would make no sense as it now stands, for there an up-down movement of the head means not "yes" but "no.")

We must forget the verbal world and its meanings when we enter the world of Mime. We cannot read its movements as though they were only so many silent words strung together into a visual shorthand. These movements develop their own dynamic. Sometimes, it is true, they can be translated by a word or a sentence, but, often as not, they "speak" out of their unique universe of discourse, one that creates space for the mime to be present in, along with the events and images of his imagination.

of a universal joint, which allows the head to swivel at a variety of angles, within, of course, defined limits. In reality, the head pivots on two vertebrae: the Atlas Vertebra and the Axis Vertebra. The Atlas allows the head to make up-and-down motions like those we make when nodding in agreement; the Axis is used to turn the head from side to side, as when we nod in disagreement. When we are in control of these pivots, the head will seem to sit on the neck as though it were a spinning top, seemingly quite able to defy the gravity of the rest of the body. In particular, one will discover that it is not necessary to move the shoulders, or even the neck, in order to agree with someone.

15

Exercises for the Head

OSCILLATION 1. Up-Down Motions. This is a series of "yeses." Take care that you move *only* the head. (1)

2. Side-to-Side Motions. The head is continually kept on a perpendicular as you make a series of "no's." Do not push the head too far to the side, otherwise you will strain your neck. (2)

3. Side Tilts. This is a series of "maybe's." The head pivots around an imaginary line drawn between the nose and the atlas vertebra. The tip of the nose will remain virtually motionless. To practice this, begin by placing a finger on the tip of your nose in order to help keep it immobile. (3)

4. Combination Moves. Combine exercises 1 and 2. The head should describe a full circle—down-side-up-side-down. Then combine exercises 1 and 3. The head describes a little circle—down-tilt-up-tilt-down.

1

2

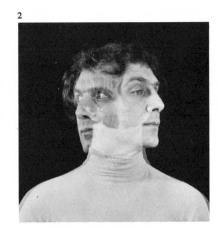

3

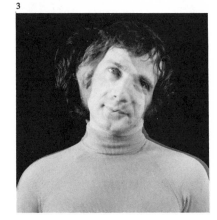

16

Mimetic Imitation

The speed at which a motion is accomplished can drastically transform its meaning. Move your head as though you were nodding in agreement, but do it in a quick series of vibrations; you will appear to be suffering the aftereffects of a blow to the head, much the way a cartoon figure is animated to look after an anvil has been dropped on its head. Or if the vibrations seem to pulsate, you will appear to be trembling with fear. One can do even more by patterning the vibrations; one can create the illusion of movement in an object other than oneself. The classic example of this is Marcel Marceau's butterfly chase. The butterfly (invisible, to be sure) flies just out of reach of Marceau's net. Rapid flutterings of his head imitate the flight of the butterfly as Marceau tries to keep up with it. The audience sees only Marceau's movements, but extrapolates from them in order to "see" the butterfly. In the butterfly sequence, we come across a basic principle of Mime: *For every specific effect, we assume there must be a cause.* If the mime duplicates the effect of watching a butterfly, his audience will find the vanishing point of his attention and fill in a butterfly. We call this physical identification with an outside, moving object *mimetic imitation*.

17

MULTIPLICATION. As we learn to master these movements, there will be a certain pleasure in putting them to some immediate use. The list of possible combinations is vast. But one must be very careful in developing such a grammar. A repertory of established expressions can become static movements, clichés that parody emotions like stock figures in a poorly done melodrama.

smile   ×   tilt   =   nostalgia or melancholy

½ smile   ×   tilt   =   irony

18

The Neck

An Edge of Vulnerability

We seem to feel a certain need to protect our neck, as though by keeping it exposed we make ourself vulnerable. Men wear collars and ties; women wear necklaces and choke collars and, sometimes, scarfs. Is all this simply a question of warmth or decoration? Or perhaps does a bit of the primordial remain with us? The faint remembrance of an enemy springing for the jugular vein?

When Mary Queen of Scots went to the axman to be beheaded, it is said, she removed a scarf she wore about her neck. This was, according to some reports, an intimate and sensual act.

In its ritual battle over territory, it is the sandpiper, I believe, that exposes its neck as an admission of defeat.

Nervous tics or twitches of the neck are good indicators of a lack of harmony. The neck muscles attempt to adjust, but to no avail, and the tics reveal the constant inner instability. A stiff neck also indicates a disinclination to find harmony, an unwillingness to find balance. Quite rightly, we call "stiff-necked" those people who are stubborn, narrow-minded, or inflexible.

The neck has charms of its own. Women as they grow older often look to their necks for the first telltale signs of age. The neck registers our fears. Ask a man a difficult question or place him in an anxious situation, and we see him take two or three quick swallows. There is not only the outside of the neck, then, but the inside of it too. (Take several swallows in rapid succession to get the feel of the inside of the neck.) Its simple function is to link the head with the rest of the body; it seems a mere pedestal for the head.

For a moment, try doing without the neck. Stand in front of a mirror and "remove" your neck; pull the shoulders up and the head down to hide it. One becomes gross and heavy and squat, even a bit stupid. Now expose the neck as much as you can. Forget about the head and shoulders. Let your neck grow. Become a giraffe, all neck. One becomes elegant; one seems more graceful, taller, and, yes, prouder. Too much neck and

19

anger   ×   neck forward   =   threat

one is in danger of looking like a snob. The grace of the neck is what we mean by carriage. It indicates the harmony and stability of the entire upper part of the body. Since the neck rests at the beginning of the spinal column, its influence is felt well down into the hips.

Depending on how we use our neck, we signal what is going on in our head. Do we lean back with our neck, exposing our Adam's apple? We show fear or surprise. Do we move our neck

proximity

listening

distance

forward with an angry expression on our face? We threaten.

In addition to these psychologically expressive uses of the neck, the mime "listens" with his neck, and "sees" with it too. The neck serves as a bellows, like those in old-fashioned cameras, to register distance and direction. But in "listening" with the neck, it is not simply that the neck moves the head, and thus the ears, in the right direction. One must feel as though the ears are in fact on the neck.

21

Exercises for the Neck

CARRIAGE 1. Forward-Back Motions. The neck carries the head back and forth. Imagine your head rests on a flat plate, like the head of John the Baptist after it had been removed from his body. All that is left for you to move is your neck. (4)

2. Side-to-Side Motions. Again the head is carried by the neck without any tilts or rotations of the head. If you have trouble doing this, place your arms around your head in the style of an Indonesian dancer. Then do the exercise again, trying to touch your shoulder with the jaw. If you still have difficulty, countertilt your head so that it leans away from the direction you are moving your head. (5)

3. Combination Moves. Combine exercises 1 and 2. The neck should describe a circular motion, first to be done clockwise and then counterclockwise.

It will be hard, but one must learn to move the neck without moving the head. (It would be a good idea to do these exercises before a mirror.)

4

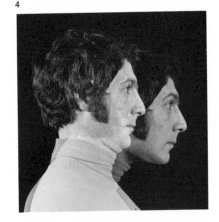

5

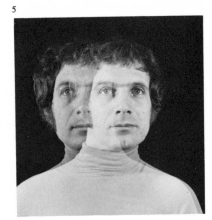

6

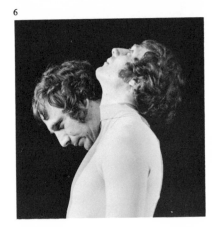

Now you can combine the neck exercises with those for the head. Adding the neck to the head exercises will add emphasis. "Yes" will become "Yes! Certainly!" (6)

22

The Trunk

The trunk is perhaps the most important part of the body. It is our center. What we do with our arms and our legs, and even our head and neck, depends upon how well we can manage our trunk. Physical acts spring from the trunk; emotions are often most deeply reflected there. When the trunk is not well used, the motion of an extremity will seem less real, less full of power. It is there that we discover the source of both the physical and the emotional energy that the body is capable of.

The trunk extends from the neck to the hips; but for our purposes, the trunk can be divided into three general parts: the upper torso, which includes the heart and lungs; the middle torso, which includes the abdomen and, roughly, the glands of our humors; and the lower torso, which includes both the waist and the hips. The division is not always absolute, given the fluidity of interaction and overlay of organs in the trunk. But we will see that the chest, for

instance, is a bit less able to translate movement into total energy, while, at the other extreme, the waist and hips are less able to register sentiments and sensibilities.

Perhaps the reason the chest registers emotions as well as it does is that it is the seat of the two organs we are most supremely conscious of—our heart and our lungs. We feel our heart beating, and we imagine it beats in every man and woman. We breathe; we feel our lungs expand and deflate. When we are in love, our heart seems to beat with noticeable swells. When we are frightened, we breathe faster and our chest shows it. Too often we make the mistake of treating our chest as though it were nothing but a billboard. If we are men, we use it to display our medals. And if we are women, we use it to express our charms.

Fair enough as far as it goes, but all of that is still to make the chest—the entire upper trunk, for that matter—far too static, something to be looked at. For the mime, the chest is much more dynamic. What matters is not its shape but its mobility and all that this mobility represents. It is the witness of our sentiment, and of our sentimentality too.

It is in the middle part of the trunk that we first feel fear. Our viscera react; our stomach pumps out juices. The center of our being seems to contract, and we shrink toward it. Joy or delight, on the other hand, appears to bubble farther from this same center. Our stomach seems to expand; it is as though pure pleasure radiates out from our solar plexus—a sun warms our insides.

The reality of a physical effort is rooted in the lower part of the trunk, despite the fact that an act may seem to be located primarily in the upper torso (for example, to pull a rope appears to need only the use of the arms and shoulders). It is true that the chest collaborates with the arms and hands to make clear the effort of pulling, but it is not the true center of our physicality—

although it may be the center of our spirit.

As the center of gravity is lowered, we find that physical energy—the merely mechanical—becomes more powerful, even more sensual. In fact, as emotions are registered farther down on the trunk, they become less refined, more raw. The trunk is moved at the waist, and the waistline is the hinge. This hinge serves to multiply the effect of a physical action. Like a lever, it provides our body with a mechanical advantage. Used by itself, the waist adds a degree of strength, although more limited than if the hips were also used. As boxers know, the twist of the torso, especially using both the waist and the hips, multiplies the strength of a punch. This is what is meant when we hear someone tell us "to get your whole body into it."

But as the center of gravity for an act takes in more of the hips, the act itself comes to seem more basically physical, instead of only mechanical. There is a difference we are all aware of between the physical as a mechanical act and the physical as a sensuous, almost sexual expression of presence.

Push against the wall with your legs together, your hips rigid, and the act will appear stiff. Push against someone with the same posture—or better yet, dance with your partner—and the act will seem timid, curiously abstract. Now add a swivel to your hips, move your legs apart to increase the leverage, and the act—or the dance—takes on a certain boldness. Sensuality permeates the act itself; the act has been renewed, given a clearer and more distinct shape. One adds more than simple energy; one adds a kind of physical humor and a degree of sexuality. The whole body vibrates. (For example, look at the rope-pulling flip sequence. Try to isolate the movements of the upper trunk. One sees the rope in the hands, but one does not *feel* the effort until one also sees the hips in motion.)

Exercises for the Trunk

CHEST 1. Forward-Back Motions. Expand the chest or rib cage as much as possible and then contract it. Your chest is a balloon to be blown up and then collapsed. Don't think of your lungs as the balloon; it is your ribs that must be expanded. Do this for a while in the normal pattern of breathing: when you breathe in, your chest expands; when you breathe out, your chest contracts. (7)

Learn to recognize the muscles in your chest that allow you to expand and contract it. Then separate the motions of the chest from the pattern of breathing. Expand your chest while you breathe out; contract your chest while you breathe in. Once you are able to counterbreathe successfully, you will know that your chest has become independent.

SEPARATING BREATHING from the motions of the chest is not meant to underrate the role of breathing. To the contrary! Breathing, like any other movement, should become as independent as possible. Then it can be used without an all too frequent waste and lack of efficiency. Although breathing is vital to any motions we undertake, breathing as such will not be given special attention in this book. We all "perform" it with relative success. No question that it could be greatly improved, but to do so requires no special Mime technique. In fact, a rather extended literature on the subject of breathing already exists. For my part, I find yoga exercises quite adequate; for me at least, the best way to start a warm-up is the yoga "salute to the sun."

2. Side-to-Side Motion. This is an expansion of the ribs on each side, first one side and then the other. In other words, move the right ribs, then the left ones. To say the least, this is a rather delicate exercise. It is really a motion that happens inside; you will probably sense it rather than see it. What counts is not that it is very visible but that you should feel it working.

3. Combination Moves. Combine exercises 1 and 2. Expand your

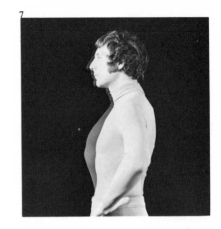

ribs, then move your right ribs, then collapse your rib cage, and finally move your left ribs. Do this in rotation, reversing the order. As in exercise 2, you will feel that you are doing it so imperceptibly that you are not doing it at all. But even if it is not at first noticeable from the outside, persist. It will pay off; sooner than you think, you will rediscover the chest from the inside. And that chest control, regardless of the amplitude or the visibility of the motions, will always be "felt"; its impact on your actions and attitudes is a basic matter.

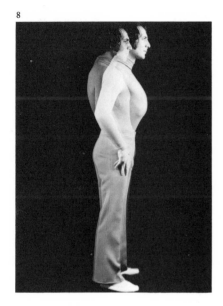

8

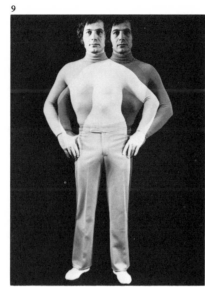

9

TORSO 1. Forward-Back Motions. For the forward motion, push the spine and chest forward; the spine will curve in. For the backward motion, chest and spine move back; the spine curves out. (8)

2. Side-to-Side Motion. The spine is pushed from side to side. To practice this, place both hands on the hips in order to keep them motionless. You may wish to give each hip a slight push in turn to counterbalance the side thrust. (9)

3. Combination Moves. Combine exercises 1 and 2. Rotate by moving smoothly from forward to side to backward to side in both directions, clockwise and counterclockwise.

HIPS 1. Forward-Back Motions. For the forward motion, move the hips forward, flattening the abdomen. For the motion back, move hips backward, flattening the spine. (Do not pivot the pelvis!) (10)

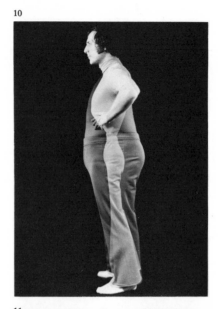

10

2. Side-to-Side Motion. The hips move sideways, curving the spine. To practice this, place both hands on the sides of the chest in order to keep it motionless. (Look down through your hands to a fixed point on the floor. If your hands and the fixed point stay in alignment, you are doing well.) (11)

3. Combination Moves. Combine exercises 1 and 2. Rotate by moving smoothly from forward to side to backward to side in both directions, clockwise and counterclockwise.

In all of these exercises, be careful not to bend at the waistline.

11

The Legs

One for the Road

Riding along joyously, since joy and wit were riding with them, Preville [a famous French actor of the seventeenth century] upon a whim decided to imitate a drunken man. While applauding Preville's imitation, Garrick [a famous English actor] told him: "My dear friend, you have missed a rather essential thing to the truth and resemblance of the drunkard you've just imitated." "What was that?" asked Preville. "You forgot to drink with your legs."

Jean Georges Noverre,
Lettres sur les Arts Imitateurs
(Paris, 1807)

The legs are the one part of the body that is in continuous contact with the physical world. The one "reality" the mime always touches is the floor he walks on. The fact that the legs make contact with the ground is a rather crucial matter. We are creatures of gravity, and our legs teach us over and over again that we are earthbound and show us our humanness.

When our animal forefathers first stood up on their hind legs, they had learned more than how to walk; they indicated their willingness and their need to defy the inertia of their universe. It is a defiance, though, that is at best tentative and limited. We discover that we must continually go through a process of compensation; we must juggle our muscles in order to retain our balance and to maintain our stability. Man is a precarious animal when he stands on his own two legs. Early in life, he finds out that he must make constant adjustments simply to stay up.

In addition to standing on our legs, we think of them primarily

29

as our means of getting from one place to another. Although we do move with them and stand on them, we also sit with them and lie down with them. For most of us, in fact, our legs are the most fretful part of the body. As we stand, we shift our weight from one leg to the other. We crook one knee or wrap one leg around the other. Sitting, we wiggle one foot, beating a rhythm we may not be conscious of; we cross and recross our legs and stretch and squirm. Even when we are lying flat, we can't let our legs be still; we scissor them, lock them together, and curl them up.

Perhaps we use our legs as much as we do because we take them for granted. We rarely think about them. But the mime cannot forget his legs. He must learn to walk again on the stage. He must relearn his connection to the ground in order to create the illusion of running, sliding, climbing, and even standing.

The legs are important for the mime because they also allow him to express character and personality. A man standing with one leg bent and crossed over the other appears to be casual, no matter what he is saying. A timid or hesitant person will often stand with his feet turned in, a shy man with one leg bent behind his calf; an impatient man will stand with one heel raised slightly as though ready to stride off, while a thoughtful man will lift one toe as though in the midst of tapping his foot to some inaudible beat.

The leg has three joints: the thigh/hip joint, the knee joint, and the ankle joint. In order to understand the importance of each joint, you might start by freezing each in turn. Freeze the hip joint and you will walk with a mince, seeming somewhat dainty and affected; you have lost the sensual power of the hips. Freeze the knee joint and you will limp; the leg becomes an object, wooden and solid. Finally, freeze the ankle joint and you will walk like an old man or woman, flat-footed and painfully.

30

THIGH 1. Forward-Back Motions. Balancing the body on one foot, swing the other foot forward and backward. (12)

2. Side-to-Side Motions. Again balancing the body on one foot, swing the foot from side to side.

3. Combination Moves. Combine exercises 1 and 2. Swing your leg to make a lazy figure eight so that you can avoid hitting the other foot.

KNEE 1. Forward-Back Motions. Balancing the body on one foot, raise the knee of the other leg and kick back and forward. (13)

2. Side-to-Side Motions. Again balancing the body on one foot, raise the knee of the other leg and kick sideways. Your thigh will twist.

3. Combination Moves. Combine exercises 1 and 2. You will do the French can-can.

12

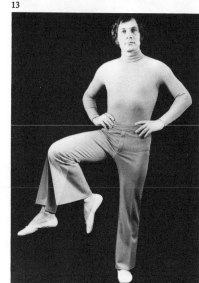

13

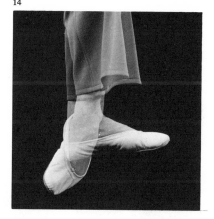

14

ANKLE 1. Up-Down Motions. Balancing the body on one foot, raise the other leg and move your foot up and down.

2. Side-to-Side Motion. In the same position as above, move your foot from side to side. (14)

3. Combination Moves. Combine exercises 1 and 2. You will make a circle with your foot.

31

Thugs pulling rope. *The Miraculous Mandarin.*

32

The Arms and Hands

To create the invisible walls of the space around him and the objects in that space, the mime must use his arms and his hands. Although this part of the body is the most flexible and free in what it can do—its joints are supple and multi-directional—it is often the most poorly used part of the body. As we have seen, when we stand still, our legs are still at work, restlessly balancing us, but our arms simply hang or fold tightly across our chest.

It is curious that we should be so limited in how we normally use our arms because it is with the arms and hands that we touch those we love, reach for what we want, stroke, pat, and caress ourselves, and patch our wounds. Through our arms we extend ourselves and our bodies into the world, gaining power over it and manipulating it. With our arms we draw other people into our space; we pull them to us or hand them objects, participating for a moment in a common action.

Our inability to use our arms well may spring exactly from this: they are invaders; they expose our intentions at the same time they penetrate other people's space. Just as importantly, they are the way we make substance of our dreams; we build with them, make with them, offer love with them. At the fingertips is a reality which we are afraid either that we cannot touch or that others will not accept. Hence our arms make us vulnerable, and we are awkward with them.

The arms, of course, accentuate or reinforce an expression or an action. We underscore sentences with our hands, give exclamation points with our clenched fists. But they can also develop and clarify what we are saying or doing, sometimes making subtle shifts in meaning.

For example, anger progresses through several stages, each stage redefined as another part of the arm and hands is put into play. In the Zero Position of anger, we begin by expanding and raising the chest; at the same time, the head tilts down and the face "closes" and darkens. In the second stage, we raise the

33

shoulders, intensifying the anger. Then we raise the elbows to the side and in back as the hands get tense and tighten; this clarifies the threat. Finally, we make material our anger; we thrust forward, producing an aggressive punch. You will observe that the emotion starts at our center—in this case, the chest—and expands outward. As more of the arm reacts, the expression of anger grows until it bursts beyond our private limits, encompassing the object of our anger.

The arm has three principal segments: the upper arm, the forearm, and the hand, connected to each other and the body, respectively, by the shoulder, the elbow, and the wrist.

Because the shoulder is the first joint between the center of our body and the arms, it takes on an important function. It is critical to expressing and releasing emotions as well as making physical acts possible. Taken together, the shoulders develop, accelerate, and magnify our meanings; but the shoulders can also be used to undercut or de-

flate our emotional involvement.

We have seen how the shoulders work to intensify anger, but let us look now at joy. We greet a friend we have not seen in a long time. We smile; we grin. By raising our shoulders, making them a part of our greeting, we increase our expression of delight. But if we freeze the shoulder joint, immobilizing the upper arm, we neutralize the action of the chest from which the emotion started. The effect is to make our face into a mask, a caricature of delight that is artificial. The shoulders' immobility denies the happiness on our face. Similarly, a shrug of the shoulders cuts off the stream of emotions from the inside, releasing the pressure slightly like the steam from a steam kettle, but not developing it or expanding upon it; the forearm does not come into play and the shoulder returns to its neutral position. The direction of the emotion has been changed; it disappears below the surface.

The elbow allows us to orchestrate our arms; because of it our arms can describe quite elab-

orate curves in the air. The elbow is a subtle joint. Besides giving our arms flexibility, it provides us with a way of carving out space for ourself. In a crowd, we use our elbows to wedge our way through, to create and carry about a little portable (and invisible) domain.

The elbow is also the solipsist's comfort. Without it, how else would we touch ourself? Hug yourself and you will begin to appreciate your elbow. It allows us to scratch an itch, brush our hair, and rub our chest. Man is a self-comforting, self-protecting creature; to satisfy those needs, he must use his elbows.

Like the shoulder, the elbow develops meaning. To see what would happen to the expression of emotions if we had no elbows, lock your arms against your side, allowing only your hands to move at the wrist. Try to be mad or happy. One can do little, except protect one's groin. As we have seen, the less amplitude the arms have (first freeze the shoulders and move only the elbow and wrist; then freeze both the shoulders and the elbow and move only the wrist), the fewer emotions we can express and the more puny and pathetic we seem to be.

Together the joints of the wrist and hands are the most supple in the whole body. Although we can touch people and objects with any part of the body, it is because of these joints that we can manipulate, taking in hand what we see. There is more, though, to the hands than that; it is not only that we can touch with our hands: our hands provide us with our *sense* of touch. They give us the palpable feel of our world.

At the end of our fingers, the nerves surface; in our palms, our pores are most immediately exposed. At our wrists, the beat of our heart is nearest at hand. (Place your wrists together, slightly cupping your fingers, and you will feel the life of your hand. Then gently touch together the tips of your fingers, from time to time barely moving each finger, and you will feel the delicate range of sensations the hand makes available.) With our hands we feel pleasure and make

it—in a primary way; and with our hands we often feel the first sensations of pain that come from touching the sharp, angular edges of objects outside us.

We use our hands to sweep the space around us in order to get familiar with it. In fact, it is through them that we are first able to become familiar and intimate with others. We shake their hands; we hold their hands; and we stroke their arms. We are allowed a public intimacy with our hands that is not allowed other parts of the body. They are the way we begin to make overtures, openly contact and connect with others.

At the same time, others begin to know us through our hands. Our inner radiance or our cool detachment flows out of our fingertips and lies on the surface of our palms. Our moods are revealed, our emotions materialized. When we clench our fists, tap our fingers, join both hands, or reach out with our palms up, we say much of what we feel. One could speak only with one's hands, and some people do.

The smaller the part of the body, the greater its power of projection.

Exercises for the Arms

SHOULDER 1. Forward-Back Motions. Thrust the shoulder forward and then backward. (15)

2. Up-Down Motions. Raise the shoulder up and pull it down. Fight the tendency to lift the elbow and to tilt the head. (16)

3. Combination Moves. Combine exercises 1 and 2. Rotate forward-up-back-down; then rotate backward-up-forward-down.

One should start these exercises with the shoulders working separately, then together, then one following the other, and finally one against the other.

ELBOW 1. Up-Down Motions. Start with the arm in a horizontal position, stretched out from the side of the body. Then bend at the elbow, swinging the forearm. This swing can vary from a small pendulum to a full circle. (17)

WRIST 1. Up-Down Motions. Flap your hand up and down. (18)

15
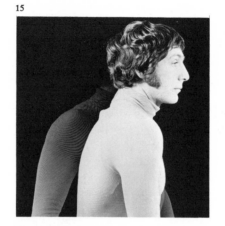

16
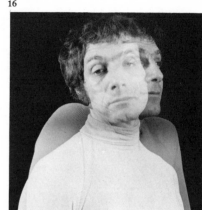

17
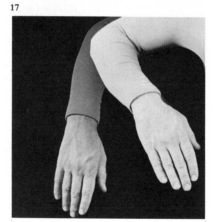

18

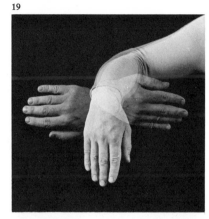

19

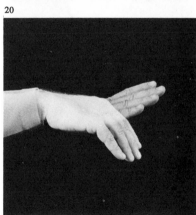

20

2. Side-to-Side-Motion. Shake your hand from side to side. (19)

3. Combination Moves. Combine exercises 1 and 2. Rotate your hand while trying to minimize the forearm motion.

Practically, the wrist will prove very useful in creating the illusion of resistance. (See page 82.) By the way the wrist carries the hand, much is revealed: the strength, delicacy, brutal force, or mannerism of the character.

HAND 1. Palm. Join all the fingers into one block and bend your hand in. Then bend your hand out: this bend will be the most difficult. (20)

2. The Fingers. Bend each finger separately. Then rotate each finger at its base without bending.

Pay special attention to the thumb. It makes manipulation possible since it can be used in opposition to the other fingers. Of course, it has some important emotional and symbolic meanings, as do some of the other fingers.

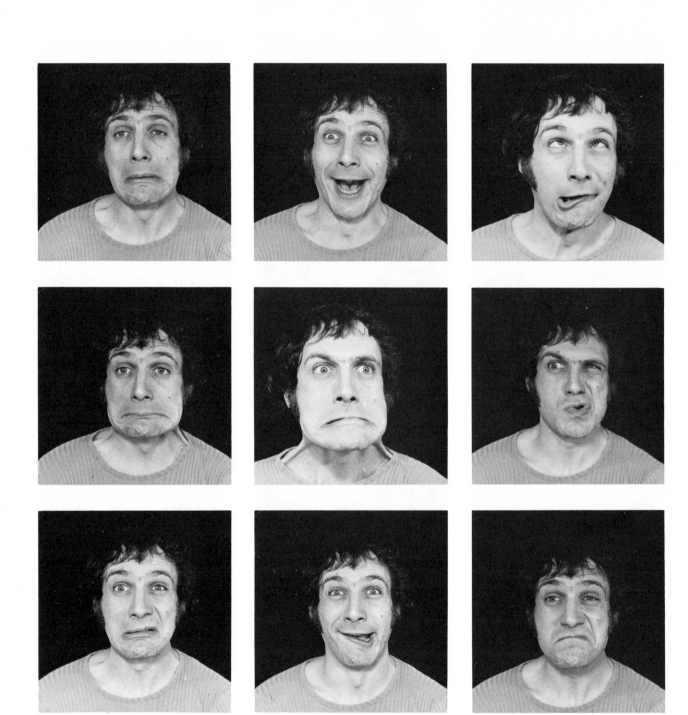

38

The Face

So far, we have learned to isolate various parts of the body. The face is the one part of the body that is isolated to begin with. Show me a man's hand without identifying it, and I will have trouble telling you its owner's name. Show me his face, and I will know him. Our face is our identity, our trade mark. No substitutes are accepted. One can imitate someone's gestures, the way he walks, the way he moves, even his voice, but one cannot imitate his face.

Even more than the head itself, the face is most totally visible; and when it is not, we feel an uneasy tension that comes from not being sure about whom we are dealing with. We want to see the eyes, the mouth, the total configuration of features that make up someone's face.

If, for instance, we are walking down the street and see someone walking ahead of us who looks familiar—that is to say, whose back and gait and motions seem like those of someone we know—before we call out, we will move up to him so that we can catch an angle of the face. The face, then, is not only the most visible part of the body, it is also the part that must be made visible.

Another characteristic that distinguishes the face from the other parts of the body is that it is always recognizable even when it is *not* in motion, while the rest of the body often is recognizable *only* when it *is* in motion. Like the other parts of the body, the face does indeed express feelings —and a quite wide range of feelings at that—but we are drawn to the face in the first place for its identity. This is an important point because it explains why the face is so totally isolated and helps us to understand that the face has its own stage with its own center of focus. Understanding this, we can see why the face is so efficient in expressing emotions: every little movement has our attention.

Most of us are relatively skilled in moving the basic facial muscles. Perhaps this is because they are the easiest to use or perhaps it is because as babies we had only our face to express emotions, so we have had a great

deal of practice. A wink, a twitch of the lips, an inflated cheek, the movement of the tongue inside the mouth, a pinched nose, and any number of other gestures are motions easy to do and easily understood by the observer.

The efficiency of the face to register meaning can, in its turn, create problems. The fact that the face allows us to say the most with the least amount of effort means that a disproportionate amount of effort can exaggerate a gesture and distort the expression of an emotion. For example, a laugh held too long becomes hysterical; the frozen smile seems artificial; lips puckered too much seem wry rather than tender. (See the discussion of the law of economy on pages 180–83.)

The mime must learn two things about his face. He must learn how to project expressions on his face by a precise control of his facial muscles; he must learn how to make the imperceptible gesture, the slight sag of his cheek muscles or the barely visible downward turn of one

Masks

Masks hide people's personalities or give them new ones. Since man discovered who he was, he has felt either the urge to hide himself or the desire to transform himself. Little wonder, then, that masks can be traced back to the beginnings of civilization. They are a part of our basic need to be disguised, a need that does not diminish despite our sophistication, our modernity, or our adulthood. Women disguise themselves when they conventionalize their faces with makeup; men disguise themselves with beards and sunglasses and hats and false hair pieces. Disguises, of course, are not bad; they liberate our imagination and our fantasies. The mask of the mime allows him to explore and develop these fantasies and to present them to his audience as each member of it might have dreamed them.

The basic white makeup mask, so classic in some Mime performances, was developed to erase the individuality of the performer. With a mask he could play a type instead of continually playing himself; it also helped enlarge his face so that it would be more readable at a distance. These two quite functional purposes of the mask clearly reinforced the mythic character of the performer: a universal type shorn of human particularities provides the essence of ritual and the essence of magic. Still, as some mimes have discovered, a flexible mask such as the makeup mask does not satisfactorily depersonalize the face.

A completely rigid mask with a fixed expression emphasizes the body and its movements. When a mime wears a rigid mask, he gives new life and meaning to his body; and he also breathes a life of sorts into his mask. From the point of view of his audience, he is not himself, not even a mime—he is a disembodied creature. It seems as though he has lent his body to the mask and created a creature not entirely human, still one quite capable of moving and touching an audience, even as plain marionettes and puppets can.

There is, then, a curious kind of transaction that develops between the fixed mask and the moving body, one that the mime tries to take advantage of. Mask and body together emphasize life even as part of the spirit is hidden. The ultimate truth about the effect the mask has—and it is true for anybody, mime or non-mime—is that it makes the body more naked, showing both its limits and its possibilities. The body can too often hide behind the face, and this is something the mime only occasionally wishes to do.

side of his mouth or the flare of his nostrils. To learn how to use the face muscles, one should work on each one independently; but it is primarily a question of refinement, of subtlety.

The exaggerated gesture is already in our repertoire. For this reason, I shall give no exercises for the face, except for some special studies of the eyes. For the most part, to learn how to use the muscles of the face, one needs only a mirror and a little dose of humorous narcissism. Pay particular attention to the mouth: it plays the most important role in modeling the face into countless masks.

The second thing the mime must learn is the connection between the face and body; these two must be in harmony. We can recall the contradictory impressions we are all left with when we see the dancer's blank face or stereotyped smile resting on his hard-working body; or an actor delivering an unconvincing speech while allowing his face to play with an overabundance of subtle gestures; or, even worse,

41

the mime grimacing pathetically to a puzzled audience.

We can understand this principle of harmony if we remember that the face is a part of the body. Most of the emotions that the face reflects are first developed inside the body at its center. Remember, the pressure of emotion moves outward. In some cases, the face and head do lead the rest of the body—for instance, when one is thinking and has caught the answer, first the head tilts, the tongue moves as though it were tasting the solution, and then the rest of the body relaxes or shudders with delight.

A few words about the eyes and their power of projection: Normally, we see an object beyond us and focus on it; the mime reverses the process since there is no object beyond him to

be seen. The mime focuses his eyes in order to project an image or the illusion of an image. His eyes concentrate on a point in space, making the external space seem hot, therefore visible, to his audience. As he squints, his lids coming closer together, he gives the impression that he is looking at something at a distance. By staring, lids wide apart, he seems

to be looking at something close at hand.

There are various obvious exercises for the eyes: looking up, looking down, looking from one side to the other, and making combinations. With a little ingenuity, one can learn how to isolate to some degree the movement of one eye from that of the other.

Depending upon the use of mask or makeup, the face can take on different meaning and reflect different ages. In this set of three pictures, the same mime plays the mandarin, a young man, and an old man. *The Miraculous Mandarin.*

2. Coordination

"What coordination!" says the enthusiastic spectator, applauding the performance, but I've never heard anybody say, "What an isolation!" Yet without an ability to isolate the various parts of the body with absolute control, one cannot have coordination. Coordination is simply the controlled combination of isolated parts.

Many of the exercises in this chapter will seem dry and somewhat mechanical, to begin with (not to mention, seeming very difficult), but they are the mime's basic chords; you must learn them before you discover their natural rhythm. Doing them, you will learn whether in fact you have mastered the isolation of individual parts; as you become more skilled, you will be able to create little compositions —some of them will amuse you because they are so absurd; some of them will suggest short sketches. (In the course of presenting these exercises, I shall explain how some of them fit into larger patterns, but you will discover your own.)

These exercises in coordina-

47

tion may be seen as a subtle form of gymnastics. The non-mime may wish to use them as simple conditioning exercises, spending ten to fifteen minutes a day on all of them; the more proficient student of mime will want to return to these exercises each day, using them to warm up. For both mime and non-mime, these exercises will help develop control over the body. By doing them, one will learn more than physical skill; one will acquire a certain grace, an ingenuity with his body that will permit him a wider range of expressive nuances.

FREE COMBINATIONS. In its way, this is the simplest, yet the most difficult and complex group of exercises to execute. It consists of combining individual isolation exercises and performing them either in series or simultaneously. In series, you will move from one part of the body to another; when they are done simultaneously, you will move several separated parts of the body at the same time, all the while keeping every other part still. Remember that most isolation exercises are in two sections. For example, the head can be moved up *and* down. To begin with, you may find it easier to do the up-down as one motion, but ultimately you should be able to do (for instance) the head-up, hip-side, shoulder-up, and then the head-down, hip-side, shoulder-down. Coordination depends upon the ability to freeze a part of the motion, pick up another motion, and then re-

turn to the original motion to complete it. Of course, as you become more adept at these exercises, you will want to increase the tempo.

As an example of a combined isolation in series, do the following: In order, move your head to the right side, then move your torso to the left, then move your shoulders up. Reverse the sequence and repeat. The following is an example of a combined isolation done simultaneously: The head tilts to the right, while the hips move to the side and the elbows move up; the body returns to its original position and the exercise is repeated. The number of possible combinations for both these exercises is unlimited. Each day create some new variations.

Coordination is a question of imbalance well balanced, as illustrated by The Waiter. *The Party*.

The Bends and Torsions

The bends teach us how to curl and unravel our body, developing our sense of our center. From it, we learn how to become a circle and a sphere. With it, we grow, shrink, expand, contract, open, and close. The mime inscribes a circle with his body by putting together the individual segments of his body; although it ultimately may be presented as a fluid motion, he never forgets that it consists of separate motions, interlocked.

Besides their technical and aesthetic value, the bends are a fundamental means of physically representing emotional pressure. (See the discussion of pressure in the chapter on "Mime of the Subject," pages 142–44.) They will allow us a wide range of expressions and physical actions. For example, the forward bend is used to indicate despair; the side bend is necessary to create the illusion of pulling; and the back bend will show the effect of a weight crushing a man.

The torsions use the same principles as the bends except that torsions move the body from side to side instead of up and down. Torsion is essentially a twist of one part of the body while freezing the other parts of the body. This means, for example, that the head and shoulder will turn to the side while the rest of the body faces forward. The torsions are a valuable way to indicate interest, involvement, or concern. First the head turns to look, then one shoulder, finally more of the body. Or it can indicate a false interest: the head turns while the rest of the body remains in its original position.

Mime Is No Easy Profession

Now I come to the pantomime. What must be his qualifications? What his previous training? What his studies? What his subsidiary accomplishments? You will find that his is no easy profession, nor lightly to be undertaken; requiring as it does the highest standard of culture in all its branches, and involving a knowledge not of music only, but of rhythm and meter, and above all of your beloved philosophy, both natural and moral, the subtleties of dialectic alone being rejected as serving no useful purpose. Rhetoric, too, in so far as that art is concerned with the exposition of human character and human passions, claims a share of its attention. Nor can it dispense with the painter's and the sculptor's arts. . . . But above all [it is] an art that would remember all things. Like Calchas in Homer, the pantomime must know all "that is, that was, that shall be"; nothing must escape his ever ready memory.

Faithfully to represent his subject, adequately to express his own conceptions, to make plain all that might be obscure—these are the first essentials for the pantomime, to whom no higher compliment could be paid than Thucydides' tribute to Pericles, who, he says, "could not only conceive a wise policy, but render it intelligible to his hearers"; the intelligibility, in the present case, depending on clearness of gesticulation.

For his materials, he must draw continually, as I have said, upon his unfailing memory of ancient story; and memory must be backed by taste and judgment. He must know the history of the world, from the time when it first emerged from chaos. . . .

Lucian, *Of Pantomime*
(second century A.D.)

Exercises for Coordination

FORWARD BEND. In sequence, the body "curls" in the following order: head, neck, chest, torso, hips. It then "unravels" back to the starting position. (21)

BEND TO THE SIDE. Each segment tilts to the side in sequence. To do the hip tilt, you will have to loosen the opposite leg. (22)

BACKWARD BEND. In sequence, bend back each element to a maximum curl. (23)

TORSIONS. In sequence, the body twists to one side in the following order: head, neck, chest, torso, hips. Then repeat, using the other side of the body. (24)

COMBINATION BEND AND TORSION. The body forms a corkscrew, bending and twisting at the same time, looking very much like the positions a discus thrower makes. (25)

21

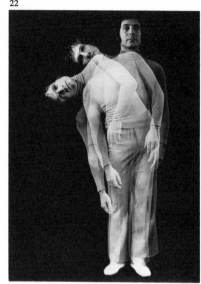

22

23

24

25

53

Undulation

Undulation (or the "wave") makes it appear that the body, or part of it, is elastic. To master this rather sensuous effect, one must have complete control over one's joints, since undulation is nothing more than a synthesis of movements caused by the regular rise and fall of one's joints. Working with the arm and hand, one can create the illusion of a serpent (see Eve-Serpent picture, page 205). Using the whole body, one can appear to be a mermaid swimming. Forward undulation is the means by which we make our audience see that we are reacting to a kick in the back; sideward undulation, to a pull.

I shall detail only the exercise for the hand serpent, but its principle and the techniques can be directly applied to both the arms and the body. Remember that you are forming a wave; like the letter S, it must have at least three segments, divided by two joints. The motion of undulation must always be smooth and progressive; one passes from one position to another without stopping.

26

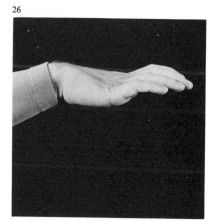

27

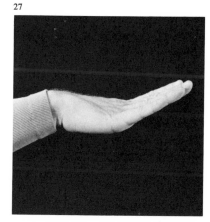

28

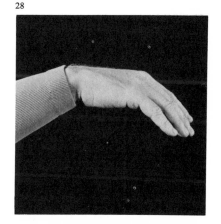

THE WAVE 1. Position of Wave. Bend your hand out. (See hand exercise, page 37.) Then, keeping the fingers together, curve them gently. This is the position of maximum tension. (26)

2. Intermediate Position. Straighten the fingers while keeping the out-ward bend of the hand. (27)

3. Position of Relax. Release the tension, allowing the hand to relax into a natural curve. (28)

You must learn to go smoothly through these three positions. By adding an up-down motion of the wrist, you will be able to whip the wave into position. For some people, this will be an easy and natural movement; for others, it will require strenuous effort. The same technique can be applied to the arms and to the body as a whole. (See exercises for the body whip, page 110.)

The Block

In *The Gold Rush,* Charlie Chaplin is standing outside the window of a cabin, hungry and cold, watching a stranger eat dinner. The question for Charlie is how to get into the warm room and, more especially, how to get something to eat. He knocks. By the time the stranger is at the door, Charlie has lain down in the snow. Of course, the stranger takes pity and tries to bring Charlie in, but he finds that Charlie cannot be bent. He appears to be a frozen slab and can be carried only like a board. This is the "block." The body, or part of it, is completely rigid.

The mime uses his ability to create the block to achieve various psychological effects. Tilting backward, the mime expresses restraint, timidity, or hesitation; tilting forward, he demonstrates readiness, courage, or the willingness to participate. (See the discussion of tendency and tilts, page 145.) To do one kind of staggering drunk, the mime must also use the block; rigidly swaying back and forth and to the side, the mime can portray the drunk's struggle with gravity and his own stability. As you will have no doubt discovered by now, keeping the body still—not to mention rigid—is very difficult. To do this exercise well, one must have mastered the ability to isolate and freeze each of the joints.

29

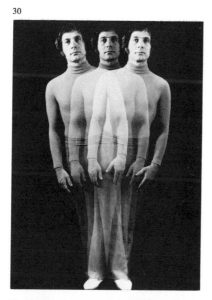

30

31

RIGIDITY 1. The Body Block, also called the "Eiffel Tower." The entire body stays rigid. Lean forward, then backward, trying to lean as far as possible without losing your balance and without breaking the rigidity (29). Try a side-to-side lean. Finally, combine the forward-backward lean with the side-to-side lean, rotating your body. (30)

2. The Block with One Loose Joint. For a forward-backward tilt, pivot the body from the hip joint forward and backward. Then, pivoting from the hip, tilt your body to the side. Finally, combine the movements into a rotation. In addition, you can loosen the knee joint to extend the possible combinations. By starting the tilt and locking the joint, you can step in any direction, mechanizing your walk. This is the technique used to play toy soldier or robot. (31)

The Collapse

To most of us, the floor is foreign. We walk on it, we can lie on it, but we don't know how to get gracefully from a walking to a lying position. Usually, we make the transition in jerky motions, as if there were something awkward and impolite in finally being on the floor. Quite rightly, in judo, the first thing one learns is how to fall. In this world one must become friendly with the floor if one hopes to survive. The collapse is one of the ways a mime moves from an upright position to a horizontal one.

In this exercise, we reverse the normal pattern of attack. Up to this point, we have learned how

to build upon each segment and joint until the whole body block was under control. To test what we build, we can now let it fall apart. Doing the collapse correctly will not only show us whether our joints are truly free but will also provide us with an excellent study of inner relaxation.

We start standing in the Zero Position with a minimum of tension. Imagine that the slight tension you are using to hold yourself upright is, in fact, all on a vertical axis running from your head, down your spine, to your feet. It is as though you are a marionette; each segment is dis-

tinct, yet all are held together by a string. Feel both the individual segments and feel the tense string that holds everything upright. Now cut the string; the collapse follows. If all the segments of your body are well placed, one on top of the other, there may be a short moment of "setting" between the cut and the collapse, as gravity takes hold.

In the collapse itself, the segments of the body will tend to fall straight down, following the line of gravity. The segments reach the floor in order and separately. The body seems to crumple. Usually, one hears the faint tattoo of the major joints hitting the floor in turn. Don't worry about hurting yourself; since each segment sits on the next, no one segment falls very far by itself.

This exercise requires a certain mental readiness, an inner relaxation, and an ability to be outside yourself and to let go—all faculties that can be acquired with a little practice.

Using the principle of the collapse, one can build a very convincing marionette. After you have fallen, reverse the process; feel the strings pulling you back up. Remember you can have strings on your arms and hands too.

Descents, Ascents, and Pivots

A curious effect is achieved if one immobilizes the upper body —from the waist to the head— while using the legs to descend, ascend, or pivot. The upper body appears to be disassociated from the floor and from its own gravity. It *is moved* rather than doing the moving itself. A man in an elevator stands passively as the elevator takes him to the next floor. In the same way, the mime descends or ascends seemingly with no conscious effort or concern; his head, shoulders, and trunk hold to whatever position they were in before the movement began. They do not become involved in the action of his legs. The descent and ascent are used to create the illusion of an elevator ride as well as to sit down in, or get up from, a non-existent chair.

Isolating the upper body while moving the legs does not look natural to the audience (and it is not natural to do); but that is a part of its charm. It is a kind of magic. With the audience's primary focus on the head, shoulders, and trunk (sometimes the mime's legs are hidden behind a low wall), the mime seems to have become a statue. In particular, this is true in the pivot, where the body appears to be revolved by a force outside itself, like a statue on a turning pedestal.

When descent or ascent is combined with the pivot, the mime can produce a spiral, which covers a wide range of expressions, from portraying a mechanical, inanimate corkscrew to presenting the sudden surprise of a violent death. In the latter, the mime turns his body away from his attacker as he falls, only to turn back and then away again, seeming to struggle with himself, with gravity, and with disbelief. In this exercise, as in so many exercises and techniques already discussed, we can see that the principle behind it is valuable and useful even if one does not use all of the elements. Once one has learned total control, one is free to take what one needs.

In practicing this exercise, one should experiment with various statue positions in order to learn how to hold whatever position one has selected while working with the legs. The secret of this exercise is to employ a continuous motion, one that is almost in slow motion. The legs should be moved in such a way as not to cause any shaking in the rest of the body.

60

Slow Motion

Slow motion is harder to master than a fast one. When a movement is done quickly, it is supported by its own momentum; all that is important is the point of departure and the point of arrival. The aim is simply to get quickly and gracefully from one to the other.

In slow motion, each moment of a movement is equally important. What counts is the continuity of the movement more than its slowness, and continuity is difficult to sustain. Once a movement is begun, one is tempted to pull it forward toward completion, and this leads to an acceleration of the movement. Or one is tempted to draw back, remaining at the beginning of the movement; this makes the movement seem hesitant or about to stop. To maintain a steady flow in the motion is delicate and requires the full attention of the body.

Once mastered, slow motion stretches the dimensions of a performance. It is indispensable to the mime; it allows him to get in and out of the dream sequences, to create the effect of instant replays, to present symbolic or accelerated growth, or even to walk on the moon.

THE ELEVATOR. Down-Up Motions. Standing on the balls of your feet, sit down on your heels and come back up in the same way. Keep your back as straight as possible. (32)

DESCENT TO THE GRAVE. Kneeling Without Sitting. Standing on the balls of your feet, bend at your knees and come down all the way to the floor; rise in the same way. The body should remain perfectly straight throughout this exercise and will lean back to avoid falling. (33)

THE WEIGHT LIFTER. The exercises above can be done with the legs apart. This in turn can be transformed by arching the back, giving the image of a weight lifter straining under the weight. (34)

Incidentally, the straight descent-ascent motions can be combined with the bend positions. It will greatly improve your balance and expand your body imagery.

32

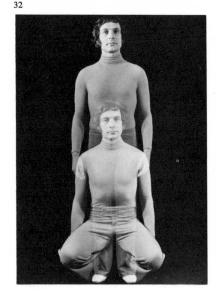

33

34

35

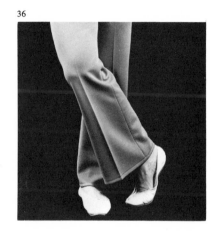

36

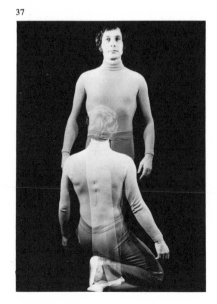

37

THE PEDESTAL 1. Half Turn. With the heel of the front foot touching the toes of the back foot on an angle, raise yourself on your toes, keeping your body straight and tense. Turn slowly and continuously into the obtuse angle formed by your feet, until your legs lock. Then reverse the motion. (35)

2. Full Turn. Cross your feet casually so that your body is balanced on the straight leg. Raise your body slightly. Then turn slowly and continuously until your legs lock. Then pivot back to your original position. (36)

You may now combine the pivots with the descent-ascent motions (37). In performing those spirals, be sure to do the combinations simultaneously or else you will lock your legs in unexpected ways. Once you can do this, you may wish to continue by combining pivots, descents, and ascents with the bends and torsions. Certainly not easy, but a good test of your skills and your body.

63

Part Two: The Illusion

3. The Movement of the Mime

Some morning, stand at a street corner and watch people cross. One man will stand vacantly, his mind filled with other business, waiting for the light to change; and when it does, it will seem as though he is being swept along with the crowd—he is not conscious of moving but has simply picked up the rhythm of everyone crossing, somewhere in the back of his mind.

Perhaps on this street corner there is a woman loaded down with packages. When she crosses, all her energy, her center of gravity, and her concentration seem to be focused on the weight she must juggle; her feet slide across the pavement, feeling their way, exhibiting a consciousness of their own. Of course, there is always someone who stands perched at the curb like a swimmer tensed for the starting gun; as soon as he can, he steps off briskly, full of purpose.

No one of the people crossing the street does so in the same way as his neighbor, and each of them would be hard put to

repeat his exact movements on demand. Most of us don't know how we move, how we prepare for each step, how we execute it, and how we end it.

It is hard to transpose these movements or any movements to the stage. The context seems so totally artificial that the movements seem unnatural. How does one pretend to cross Times Square in the middle of an empty stage? The actor has a plot, a stage setting, sound effects, and perhaps some other actors with him to help him get from one corner to the other. The dancer has music to tie together his movements; his individual movements, strictly speaking, mean less than the total effect.

The mime cannot afford to mystify his audience with any movement; gratuitous motions will squander his credibility with his spectators and confuse them too. Confusion is so easy because there is no sub-text to help the audience understand what it is seeing. His clothing says nothing; and, for the most part, he has nothing with him. Only by moving does he make sense of the empty space he is in; only by his moving do we know who he is; only by his moving do we know where he is. On stage, the mime behaves in a certain way that is clearly his own.

To have mastered the mechanics and combinations of isolation is not in itself enough to be a mime. No matter how elaborate or artful one's combinations are, one will remain only a trickster. One's audience may sit amazed, but it will not be in-

formed. The mime learns how to articulate his movements, giving each a certain logic, a certain recognizable shape. To give visualizable shape to each movement, the mime sees each movement as composed of three distinct elements: pressure, immobility, and clic. Each of these elements provides him with a way of setting the movement and helps him place it in a larger context of action and conflict. He will watch people in the street differently than we normally do. He will observe the relative lack of pressure in one man, the tension between moving and not moving in another, and the instance of motion in a third. He will watch others so that he can learn to watch himself, in order to give shape and substance to what he does.

Pressure

A Perfect and Delectable Dancing

Over Syracuse (a great and ancient city in Sicily) there reigned a cruel tyrant called Hiero, which by horrible tyrannies and oppressions brought himself into the indignation and hatred of all his people, which he perceiving, lest by mutual communication they should conspire against him any rebellion, he prohibited all men under terrible menaces that no man or woman should speak unto another, but instead of words they should use in their necessary affairs countenances, tokens, and movings with their feet, hands, and eyes, which for necessity first used, at the last grew to a perfect and delectable dancing. And Hiero, notwithstanding his foolish curiosity, at the last was slain of his people most miserably.

Sir Thomas Elyot, *The Boke Named The Governour* (London, 1531)

As you sit in your chair, reading this book, your body is exerting pressure. Gravity is pushing us down; pressure is keeping us up. The mime has an acute sense of the pressure in his body; it is like a field of energy that envelops him. He feels it at his center, and he feels it at the edges of his flesh. When you stand in Position Zero, you will feel every part at ease. The energy within your body is equally distributed and the body feels its unity. Pressure is a way the body expresses this unity and registers harmony. It is a comfortable feeling.

To get in touch with the pressure of your body, concentrate on the lower part of your body. Start at your hips and move down through your legs to your feet. You will feel the gentle weight of each part of the body. The energy used to support the weight of your body is pressure.

Sometimes when we wake up in the morning, we lie there in bed, quite happy, but unable to move; the weight of our body is so equally distributed that it is beyond our imagination or our will to disturb it.

69

If you are sitting down and you decide to kick one leg up, the act will require an increment of energy. You will have to exert pressure (through your muscles) to your leg and to the parts of the body that surround it. Pressure is two forces in one: it is both the force we use to sustain or maintain a position (we call this Pressure Zero) and the force we need if we are to move from one position to another.

It should be clear that the mime thinks of the concept of pressure in a way very different from the way a physiologist or a physicist thinks of it. This is not strange since the mime is trying to discover the way to create an effect; the components of the illusion are what he is after.

To the mime, pressure becomes virtually a tangible sensation, verging on the sensual. He is conscious of it when he moves and when he is still: to feel it, he must touch his body with his inner senses. It is his presence that he becomes conscious of. He feels himself as a three-dimensional force with himself at the center of it. A paradox perhaps,

but a real and possible state of feeling too. For these reasons, pressure is something more than physical or physiological.

Pressure is a reflection of emotions and moods. We *can* feel happiness; we *can* feel sadness. And the shape of our body changes to match these feelings. The mime takes this into account; he changes his physical expression of pressure to fit the hidden emotions of the imaginary personality he is creating.

We can see around us many examples of this balance between physical and psychological pressure. Remember the last time you were depressed, or someone you know was depressed. The body became deflated, the chest drawn in; the shoulders were hunched, and the head lowered. The body almost seemed to bend into a ball. On the other hand, remember the moment of someone's joy. Joy radiated out; his posture and his skin were more trim, more taut. It is what we mean when we say, "He's brimming over." Emotions appear to flow outward from the center of the body—or appear to collapse

back into it, as if they were trying to fill a void.

Centering both physical and emotional pressure is critical to a mime's performance. Take the example of greeting friends at a distance. As we recognize them, we do not simply raise our arms and wave a hand. We thrust out our chest as though it too were expanding to meet them. We feel expansive. We *are* expansive. A simple gesture with arms raised but with the chest remaining static would not look true. Friends who greet us that way are not friends. They have merely delivered a social reflex.

Rather than considering motions as a series of separate mechanical acts, the mime tries to rediscover the source of the movement. The pressure that makes his chest expand and his arms move out is one of elation, one that he places at his center and lets expand outward, into his face and to the ends of his fingers. Done in a continuous and smooth manner, it unifies the whole body, not only making the movement seem "true" but making it seem graceful.

70

Immobility

Young man freezes after having been kissed by a girl. *The Miraculous Mandarin.*

Short of death or coma or deep sleep, there is no true immobility. And even death, coma, or sleep is less immobility than a state of collapse. The immobility we are concerned with is a conscious and active process, not a passive condition. As we have already seen in the isolation exercises, it is quite difficult to try not to move. The struggle with gravity continues. A war goes on in the body in which hundreds of tiny pulls and pushes work together to produce an apparent serenity. The student of Mime quickly learns that for every position there is a certain pressure that will achieve immobility in that position. Clearly, then, he must not only learn a position but must also learn the pressure required to hold it. This is how he achieves immobility.

The student of Mime will discover the sad truth that immobility is only an effect. While in it, he will be doing a great deal of work, although it will seem to his audience that he is doing nothing. It will look easy to those who are watching (and it *should* look easy), but it is perhaps the

hardest skill the mime must learn.

In its way, immobility is the essential skill in the mime's art. It is the moment *just before* movement, and it is the moment *just after* movement. Hence, even in its immobile condition, the body is ready to function. Just before a movement, an imperceptible amount of pressure is added. This is what we normally call tension.

Immobility is secured by the efficient use of pressure (neither too much nor too little). Tension is the maximum amount of pressure that can be used without moving the body and breaking the immobility. In a state of tension, the body is prepared for what it must do next without losing control over what it is doing now. You can see why immobility assumes such a high degree of both physical and mental consciousness.

A variation of immobility is the freeze: here a continuing movement is suddenly stopped. Movement is crystallized. It is a rich and powerful counterpoint to the mime's actions. Used well, it can add texture to movements because it refocuses the attention of the audience. Both time and motion have been stopped, and the audience feels as though it has been brought closer to the event. Now the audience can almost reperceive what it has just seen and can anticipate what is to follow.

The freeze is also an expression of power since it so efficiently gathers up energy, implying the sudden release of a yet to be performed movement. A threatening fist held high in the air promises an explosion—one we can sense if not hear—before the fist has landed. We flinch in expectation.

The Clic

To Do All Things with Order . . .

In a Word, a Pantomime to deserve that Name, must be every Thing exactly, and do all Things with Order, Decency, and Measure, like himself without any Imperfection; have his Thoughts perfectly composed, yet excel in a Vivacity of Mind, a quick Apprehension, and deep Judgment; and his Applause must be the necessary Consequence of his Performance, in which every Spectator must behold himself acted, and see in the Dancer, as in a Glass, all that he himself used to do and suffer.

John Weaver, *A History of Mimes and Pantomimes* (London, 1728)

As we have seen, the immobile body gathers up pressure to the point of tension and then it moves, in much the same way that a coiled spring stores energy before the release. This instant of release is the clic, a physical accent that marks the body's passage from immobility into movement. Slightly less apparent but no less true, the clic is also the moment when the body turns from movement back into immobility.

One does not always see the clic in a mime's performance, but one feels it. It should be there like a form of subliminal punctuation, a key means of enhancing a performance. It outlines the beginning of a movement and puts into highlight its completion. When it is missing, one notes that something is wrong. Like punctuation, it is most noticeable when absent. Beginnings seem less crisp; stops are less sharp. Somehow a performance is less "readable."

The mime who does not weave the clic into the basic structure of his movements may well dis-

73

cover that he has lost a crucial clarity. The clic is often the difference between a movement that is merely comprehensible and one that is distinctly credible.

Although we dwell on clics here, not all movements need pronounced clics. In many cases, the clic will be merely the subtle underpinning of a movement. But sometimes they are creatively played with: for example, a false start or an exaggerated clic after one has been taken by surprise and hit below the belt and the pain suddenly registers. The clic covers a quite wide range of intensities, from the imperceptible to the extreme explosion. It can include the whole body or only a small part of it.

To learn how to do the clic, we must return to the moment when the pressure of immobility

has built up to extreme tension without being released into movement. At the release, the muscles contract. It is this physical contraction that produces the impression of a condensed outburst, a little shock. (Yet another paradox: a contraction produces an outburst! But muscles, after all, cannot expand; they can only contract and be released.)

Practically speaking, the mime accentuates his starts and then stops: examples are the initial outburst of the chest (clic!) in a burst of joy, and the sharp stop (clic!) of the accusing finger. (For a discussion of how the clic creates the illusion of the basic actions, see page 94. In the meantime, look carefully at the rope-pulling flip sequence to see the clic in operation.)

4. The Mime of the Object

Through his movements, the mime creates two worlds. In one, he creates the illusion of a physical world that exists around him, in which there are objects for him to discover, people to meet, and in which he walks and runs and finds a place for himself to stand. We shall call his ability to create this outer world from empty space: the Mime of the Object. The second world is the one in which he himself is the subject, to begin with on a private stage, quite invisible to his audience. On that stage are his feelings, emotions, and the basis of the character he is creating. He must find a means to project this private space and its values outward so that it can be readily apparent to his audience. This we call the Mime of the Subject.

Although in this and succeeding chapters we shall take each of these kinds of Mime movement in turn, it is worth noting now that there is finally no true way to keep them separate, nor should there be. Even the most impersonal and objective movement reflects a certain style and a certain personality. A drunk

75

will pick the same flowers differently from a dandy; one man will hold an empty box differently from another. On the other hand, feelings must have their objective correlatives. The objective, tangible world often provides us with the cause of our feelings; more importantly, it gives shape and substance to them. A man in love will feel and touch the world differently; a woman who is proud will walk differently than she does when she is sad or even happy.

Fiddler in the *shtetle*. *The Village*.

76

Contact and Touch

Before we can establish an environment for others to see, we must come to know it for ourselves. We must learn to make contact with it; in some way, we have to touch it. But we need not limit ourselves when we think of touching the world. Of course, there are our hands to use, but there are also other senses that will allow us to know the feel of reality. One may touch with one's sight, with one's hearing, or the sense of smell and taste. The whole body itself speaks of the shape and substance of this world. (". . . you see how this world goes," says Lear to blind Gloucester. Gloucester's reply captures a truth: "I see it feelingly"—and it is an amazing truth indeed. Yet in the complexity of Lear's mind there is another truth too: "What, art mad? A man may see how this world goes with no eyes. Look with thine ears." Somewhere in the center of this exchange is the essence of what a mime must know and what he helps his audience to rediscover for itself.)

When the mime touches with his eyes and ears, as well as with his hands, the objects and people he touches seem to touch him back. They re-create his senses. And he needs these senses, moving as he does among so many things that are, to begin with, invisible, that are so soundless, odorless, tasteless, and without apparent form.

The truth is that we all move in this same invisible world, but the difference is that the mime has no illusions about it. He is quite free to make reality because he does not inhabit our waking world. He may exchange one sense for another or play with the laws of common sense. He may see by touching, and he may think by tasting. In particular, it is his power to touch things at a distance (no matter what sense he uses) that gives him the magical ability to make contact with a world so that his audience may be in touch with it too.

TECHNIQUE OF THE TOUCH. According to the habits of our Newtonian universe, when we touch something, we stop. For example, I raise my hand and

then bring it crashing down on the table. When my hand hits the table, it will stop! The mime takes this principle into account, but reverses the order of things. He brings his hand down and stops, and then the table exists. To make this illusion work, the mime must depend upon the logical inclinations of his audience, even though the logic is reversed. If for every cause there is an effect, why then, for every effect there must be a cause. This is the principle of inference on which the illusion of Mime relies so heavily.

Let us look carefully at how this illusion is created. When the mime has reached the space that he intends the imaginary object to occupy, he sharply checks his movement. He extends his arm in front of him, then stops his motion with a clic of his hand. This clic stop *is* the contact! The imagined object *begins* where the movement of the mime ends. It is really very simple; the secret of the illusion is in a good stop, in a stop with a good clic.

The effects of a good stop can be most subtle and amusing, especially as one complicates the levels of contact. For example, to mime leaning casually against a mantel with your elbow, immobilize the elbow as though it has been stopped by the mantelpiece while relaxing the wrist so that it can dangle freely. This combination of rigidity in one part of the body and total relaxation in a connected part bespeaks absolute nonchalance. (Remember in trying this to pivot your hips because they too will be a part of this nonchalance.)

Another elaboration of this effect is to mime half-sitting at a stool at a bar: one foot is on the ground; your behind is perched on the edge of the stool; and one leg dangles in the air, while one arm rests partly on the edge of the bar. The arm-wrist action is the same as it was for the mantel lean; but in this case the thigh and behind are immobilized, while the knee away from the bar is relaxed, allowing the foot to swing freely. As you can see, the illusion of contact is often a blend of rigidity and relaxation. It will look like nonchalance to the audience, but it will demand a very active concentration on your part.

78

38

39

40

The Box and The Globe. (39, 40)

THE STOP 1. Move your arms around in the air, stopping your hands frequently with a sharp clic to establish points of contact. Learn how to do a good clicky stop. (38)

2. Now learn how to create *one* surface for all the points of contact by always stopping your hands in the same plane in space. (This is the principle of *fidelity* of plane; a mime can mime nothing without being able to be faithful to the planes he is creating.) Try to cre-

ate a flat vertical surface in front of you—the wall, for instance. Then try to create a flat horizontal surface—a table.

THE SHAPE. The next stage in developing the illusion of contact is to introduce the notion of shape. An aspect of knowing the shape of an object is that one is able to feel its contours. Therefore practice stroking surfaces, all the while remaining faithful to their planes. Try first an imaginary wall, then an imaginary table. Finally, com-

bine your vertical and horizontal moves so that you can fondle an imaginary box. (39)

Exercise your imagination and your skill by touching and stroking any imaginary surface or volume—for instance, a globe, cone, cylinder, etc. Make such curves and right angles in the air as strike your fancy, but remember to honor the fidelity of planes and to use the clic when coming in touch with these planes. (40)

The Muscle Man

Let us say that an object rests on the floor in front of us. We do not know how much it weighs, but on the basis of its size and what we know of its mass (that is, whether we think it is empty or solid and what we think it is composed of), we are tempted to guess at its weight. Our muscles flex in anticipation. But, as we all know, this is not a foolproof method. We can probably all recall a time when we picked up something, bracing ourselves for a great weight, only to have the object prove virtually weightless. Weight is deceptive, a fact that works in favor of the mime. And it is relative too. The strong man at the circus picks up a hundredweight as though it were a feather, but the rube who saunters up afterward staggers under it.

Weight and Resistance

When we say that an object is heavy, we mean that it strongly resists our efforts to lift it or move it or push it. If it is difficult to move, the object itself seems to be resisting us. So, for all practical purposes, the weight of something is the same thing as its resistance. This is not an intricate observation, but it is a useful one. The mime must find a way of indicating weight where there is no weight, just as he had to learn how to indicate surface where there was no surface. By exchanging the stop for a touch, he created surface; now by exchanging resistance for weight, he can create mass.

We see in these kinds of exchange an essential quality of the mime's imagination. He searches for equivalencies that will allow him to represent *what is not* by using the physical reality of his body. He must uncover the logic of the world he wishes to make visible so that he can translate it into the movements of his body. In the case of the weight of things, the idea that everything resists being moved shows him how to deal with the problem of moving imaginary objects.

Let us say that a mime wants to push away a box he wishes you to believe is in front of him. How does he go about it? He can touch it, stopping his hands at its planes. He can run his hands over its surface, projecting its size and even its shape. All of that will give you a sense that something does indeed exist.

But what about its weight? Since we have seen that weight is resistance, the mime shows us that the box resists his efforts to move it. With his hands resting on the plane of his imaginary box, he pushes; but he does not push beyond the plane he has created, unless he wants to show that the object is moving. We see him strain; we see the resistance build up in him. He has put his body under great pressure, which translates to us as great exertion. We know that the box must be heavy, at least for him.

The mime has incorporated resistance into himself. He resists himself in order to produce the effect of external resistance. Once more the mime asks his audience to apply the principle of inference. He resists, and the object appears to be resisting him. We see effort, and we are ready to visualize the cause of that effort.

The effect of resistance in the body is achieved by a slowdown of the normal movement. The purpose of the exercises in this section is to acquaint you with the fundamental techniques necessary for such a slowdown. (In the sections on manipulation, pages 83–89, and on the action on objects, pages 94–104, we shall consider other aspects of the concept of resistance.) For now, it is important to remember that every movement should start with a clic; it is the effect of a clicky beginning to a movement, added to its slowdown, that creates the illusion of resistance.

Exercises for Resistance

THE FLIP. The mime must not forget that everything—absolutely everything—has some resistance. In this set of exercises, we shall concern ourselves with the resistance and variable density of the air around us.

Give the atmosphere various weights; make it seem thicker and thinner. Much of the credibility of this movement will depend upon the clic of the wrist. As the hand is moving in one direction, the wrist clics *against* this direction, thus changing the general direction. A good way to do this exercise is to think of your hand as a paintbrush and your arm as the handle.

1. Moving up. The handle moves upward, pressing the brush on the wall; the brush bends and drags after the handle, smearing the paint in the process.

2. Moving down. Flip! A sharp change in direction. Do not scoop the air at the top of your stroke, rounding off the change. The handle moves downward; the brush must flip to follow.

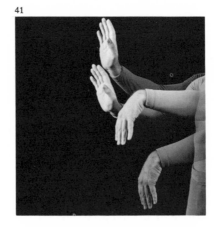

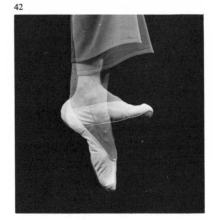

Do this several times. Feel the resistance of the heavy air and the drag it creates. With each change in direction there is a new movement marked by a clic, followed by a slowed-down motion. (41)

3. After you have gotten control over an up-flip-down motion, do a side-flip-side motion, smearing the air sideways.

4. Combine the up-flip-down with the side-flip-side.

5. Finally, try a coordinated up-down motion using both hands. One arm moves down while the other goes up. (This is quite tricky!)

As we can see, the *flip* is the most visible manifestation of this technique for resistance. This brisk change of direction need not be limited to the hand. All the extremities of the body are capable of doing a flip. Eventually one can learn to perform the flip at almost any major joint, but the feet and head (as well as the hands) are most suited for it.

6. Move the feet in water. The leg moves to the right, flip! The foot, slowed down by the water, tilts to the left and trails after the leg. (42)

82

Manipulation

Every day, almost continuously, we pick things up and put them down; we turn knobs, insert keys into locks, and perform all the assorted activities of living and surviving. Much of the time, we don't think about what we are doing; we have done these things so often, they have become habits. Who has to think of how to pick up a glass or how to hold a coffee cup or how to screw the top on a jar? But when we were babies, this was all quite strange to us.

Every object had its individual problems; each was in some way unique. The mime must return to that first sense of the palpable uniqueness of objects. If we think about it, consciously think every time we pick up an object, we will be struck by how incredibly adroit we are when we handle objects. It's really quite tricky, even manipulating the real thing.

What about handling non-existent ones? An advantage, of course, to working with the invisible is obvious—there is no fear of breaking anything. However, the mime novice has an-other fear. He fears the invisible itself; he hesitates in front of the void. But it is precisely this empty space that is his "material." He must learn how to mold it, shape it, lift it, and fondle it. It is space that he learns to manipulate, in the way he once learned how to manipulate a glass or his knife and fork.

Since space is what he is learning to handle, he must practice on space. When he was a child, he did not learn how to pick up a fork and how to use it by *pretending* to pick up a fork; similarly, he will not learn how to pick up an imaginary fork by picking up a real one. This is a common mistake beginners in Mime make; they handle real objects—getting the feel of them, as it were—in hopes that they will ultimately be able to put reality down and pick the imaginary up. This approach will not do if we wish to re-create objects, and not merely simulate them. To succeed, we shall have to do more than the real-life motions; we must learn how to compensate for the absence of the real objects.

83

TECHNIQUE OF MANIPULA-TION. In chronology, here is what happens when we handle objects: (1) *The Approach.* In real life, the approach to the object is a transitory moment of little consequence, a rather automatic gesture. For the mime, the approach is a very conscious moment during which he *announces* the object. It is charged with intentions, even emotions; it reflects hesitation or decision. Hence, the approach is a crucial moment of manipulation that can spell the difference between craft and art.

The approach is usually the domain of the hand, since the hand is most often what makes contact with an object. Of course, the rest of the body is involved, especially the eyes, which appraise the object and first take it in.

Early in his approach, the mime opens his hands in anticipation. The approach itself is arched, describing a curve. Even at this point, the mime can be quite expressive. Variations in the "openness" of the hand and the degree of arch in the ap-

---

What Do You Mean by That?

. . . Panurge raised his thrice mighty codpiece into the air with his left hand, and with his right drew from it a piece of white ox-rib and two pieces of wood of the same shape . . . which he placed symmetrically between the fingers of that hand. These he struck together, making the sort of noise that the lepers of Brittany make with their clappers—but it sounded better and more harmonious. At the same time, with his tongue contracted in his mouth, he hummed joyously, all the while looking at the Englishman [by name, Thaumaste]. By which sign the theologians, doctors, and surgeons imagined Panurge to infer that the Englishman was a leper. But the counsellors, lawyers, and canon-lawyers thought that in so doing he wished also to imply that some kind of human felicity lay in the leprous state, as Our Lord once affirmed.

The Englishman was not alarmed by this and, raising both his hands aloft, held them in such a way as to close his three master fingers in his fist and poke his thumbs between his index and middle fingers, with his little fingers extended at full length. . . .

Whereupon Panurge silently raised his hands and made this sign: He put the nail of his lefthand forefinger onto that of the thumb, making as it were a ring in the space between them and clenched all the fingers of his right into his fist except the forefinger, which he repeatedly thrust in and drew out of the space between the two others of his before-mentioned left hand. Then he stretched the fore and middle fingers of his right, keeping them as far apart as possible, and pointing them at Thaumaste. . . .

Thaumaste began to tremble and grow pale, and made him this sign: With the middle finger of his right hand he struck the muscle of the palm beneath the thumb, then put the forefinger of his right hand into a ring formed with his left; only, unlike Panurge, he put it in from below, not from above.

Then Panurge struck one hand against the other and blew in his palm. After which he once more thrust the forefinger of his right hand into the ring made by his left, pushing it in and drawing it out several times. Then he stuck out his chin and looked intently at Thaumaste. By which the spectators, who understood nothing of these signs, realized that he was silently asking Thaumaste: "What do you mean by that?"

François Rabelais, *Gargantua and Pantagruel,*
translated by J. M. Cohen (Baltimore:
Penguin, 1955)

proach tell a great deal about the character and the mood of the would-be manipulator. For example, the approach will seem lyric or thoughtful if the open hand describes an ample curve. It will seem sneaky or timid if the hand remains almost clenched and darts straight for the object, as if surreptitiously.

(2) *The Take.* Despite the importance of its function, the take should offer us the least problem of all of the concepts we have considered. It is so much a part of our life. Let us realize that the take is a combination of touching and shaping an object. At the end of the approach, we touch and close our hand on the object, simultaneously establishing our contact and its shape. Most important here is the element of fidelity, for once again we must remember to honor the planes of the object.

I grab an apple, a certain apple with a certain size. In holding it, I have to maintain its size and shape. And if I should start to eat it, I reinforce the illusion by decreasing the size of my grasp with each corresponding

85

bite I take. Fidelity to an object and to the changes it undergoes sustains the illusion and builds up the credibility of the invisible world the mime presents.

In addition to fidelity, one must keep in mind the attitude of the hand during the take. Although the mime adapts the shape of his hand to the shape of the proposed object, this can be done in countless ways.

I wish to take a flower. Should I do so with two fingers, or three or four, or with all five? Should I lock my fist around its stem? Or use only my thumb and index finger? And if only my thumb and index finger, should I let the rest of my hand remain open or closed?

Each gesture will tell something different, both about the flower and about the character being played by the mime. Generally, the attitude of the hand can be used to register the function of an object, its weight, and even its texture. At the same time, it will reflect the mime's intentions toward the object, his care or neglect, his greed or largess.

(3) *The Release*. Paradoxically, the most important element in creating the illusion of an object is the release, the moment when the mime opens his hands and leaves the object.

I take a glass. The audience sees my hand around its imaginary shape. I carry it to my lips and drink. All the while, the audience understands that I am holding a glass. Then I put the glass down and release it. The imaginary glass stands alone, and the audience sees it! An invisible object has shape. (In fact, if I try to pick up this same glass but take it from a different point in space, the audience will think it a mistake or that I have selected another glass. This is a confusion to be avoided; one is either not in control of one's space or one is simply indulgent.)

Devil drinking. *L'Histoire du Soldat*.

87

Exercises for Manipulation

MANIPULATION exercises are limited only by the number of objects one can manipulate; and the number is unlimited, each object requiring an exercise peculiar to it. Yet most of the problems of manipulation can be solved by mastering one series of exercises done around one object. The one which offers the best range of possibilities is the simple stick. Even here, the exercises I suggest do not exhaust all the possibilities, and you will want to think up your own.

THE STICK 1. Ladder your hands up the invisible stick. Take the stick vertically in one hand; release your hold and then grab with the other hand. Continue this process, passing the stick from one hand to the other. (43)

2. Next do the exercise outlined in 1, but with the stick held horizontally. A valuable variation of this is to change the position of each hand at each grab, from an upper-grab with the knuckles down to an under-grab with the knuckles up. This is an important variation; it forces the hands to make each re-approach with care, so that one does not pass through the stick. (44)

3. With both hands on the stick, move it around. Fidelity is crucial here. Fidelity to the object in this case means the fidelity of one hand to the other. The space which separates the two hands and their relationship to each other must remain constant throughout the movement. (45)

43
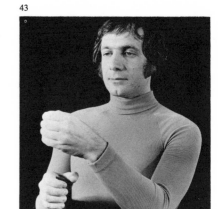

88

44

45

4. Combine all of the preceding exercises with an outburst of virtuosity as though you were a performing majorette.

Needless to say, by practicing the take in the above exercises, you will also be practicing the approach and the release. One cannot grab a stick without getting hold of it; and if one does not release it, the stick will begin to look like so much plastic spaghetti. You may wish to practice approach and release with other objects—small perfume bottles, big jars, pieces of chalk, whatever appeals to you.

89

Compensation

Some of the most striking effects of illusion that the mime can achieve are based on the technique of compensation. Let us say we have created a wall. We have used touch to establish its existence, although only a partial sense of its existence. The wall is long, and the wall is high. Patting it is not sufficient to create its total reality. So we want to walk along the wall, leaning against it, in order to feel its textures, to see if there are any openings in it, or simply to discover how long it is, how high it is, and what directions it goes in.

How does one go about making a solid continuity? The wall is immobile; the mime is mobile. The mime creates a relationship between his movements and the fixed wall he is probing. He cannot just walk along the wall; he must be in contact with it. He is like a blind man who sees no wall unless he is touching it or has already touched it. Compensation consists in respecting this relativity between the mime's movements and the fixed object he is moving in terms of.

Why is compensation necessary? And how does one do it? Let us look at the wall again. I go up to a wall and put my hands on it and then decide to take one step to the left. If it were a real wall, my hands would drag along with the rest of my body, moving the equivalent of one step to the left. In Mime the trouble is that my movement becomes the focus and the wall is de-emphasized. In seeing me move, the audience will not see me move *along* the wall. So while I move to the left, I must keep my hands on the spot I have already touched—the spot that has already been created in the audience's imagination. To do this, I push my hands to the right *at the same time* I move to the left.

Compensation is a double movement in which one motion negates the other. The final effect is that my hands remain on the same spot of the real space on that unreal wall. I may then move my hands along the wall, bringing them closer to my body, touching the wall, feeling it, making all this new space seem real by my contact.

Exercises for Compensation

THE WALL 1. Forward-Backward. Put your hands on the imaginary wall in front of you; your arms are straight. Take a step forward, approximately one foot, and at the same time move your hands back toward you by one foot. This will bring you closer to the wall. Now move away from the wall: take one step back and extend your arms; you will be back where you started. (46)

Try this set of exercises, taking more than one step each time. After you have mastered this movement on the vertical wall, do the same movements on the horizontal, as though you were working over an imaginary table.

2. Side-to-Side. Your hands are on

the wall in front of you; and you are close to it, so your arms are flexed. Take a step to the left as you push your hands one foot to the right. Reverse these moves so that you are back at your starting position. (47)

Repeat these movements for the other side: one step to the right as your hands move one foot to the left. Try these exercises, taking more than one step each time. Now move side-to-side over a table.

THE TABLE. For this illusion, put your hands on an imaginary table in front of you, which is at waist level. Stand up on your toes (about three inches) as you lower your hands three inches. Reverse this exercise so that your hands are

46

47

92

48

49

in their original position and you are standing with your feet flat on the ground. Next bend your knees and sit down one foot lower than your standing position with your hands raised one foot. You should also try to squat lower, perhaps all the way down to the floor. (48)

THE POLE. Combine the various moves. You are now, for instance, in a subway, holding on to a vertical handrest pole. Play with it in several ways: hold the pole with one hand, go toward it, away from it, and from side to side. Exchange hands. Stand up; sit down. Turn around the pole. Putting the elements of this exercise together, you will look like someone taking a very crowded and bumpy subway ride. (49)

THE LABYRINTH. The idea behind this exercise is to shift from one fixed or already established point of space to another—for example, walking along a wall. This can be done in two ways. In the first, juxtapose a series of side moves (see exercise 2), stopping after each step. In the second, run your hands along the wall, one after the other, as though they were "walking" on the side of the wall. At the same time, you should be walking non-stop, continuing a compensation between both feet and hands. By changing directions, one can create an imaginary labyrinth. Try this same exercise on a table, making a horizontal maze.

Actions on Objects: Push and Pull

There may seem to be countless ways to act on objects, but when we come right down to it, there are only two basic actions: pushing and pulling. Every other act is a variation of one of these two. What about breaking or bending something? Or what about a gentle squeeze or a much more daring and rather splendid smash? These two are only variations on a single theme: in each, pressure is applied according to the requirements of the action, each at a different speed. The basic act is the push, despite the elaborations and the effect.

Push and pull themselves have a common denominator: they both are the means by which we displace objects, be it by moving or throwing or taking or carrying something from one place to another. What primarily distinguishes push from pull (aside from the direction of energy) is that the push does not require a take or a grab, while the pull does demand that we are able to grasp the object.

There are four elements to the act of displacement, used in both push and pull: positioning, clic, resistance, and compensation. Each one of these has been discussed in an earlier context, but now we shall see how in a specific combination and in a particular order they will enable us to push and pull at will.

Positioning includes both the touch and the take as well as the gathering of energy—what we called the development of pressure into tension. The instant of outburst in which the energy is directed against the object is the clic. As the weight of the object brakes the energy of the movement, resistance becomes a dominant factor. During the whole process, the body compensates by moving away from the direction of its energy—much like the recoil of a gun.

Miming and Mouthing

A mime walks onto his stage, empty-handed and mute. It is not long before his hands seem full of objects. We do not find it hard to imagine him sitting down in a chair on an empty stage. But how does a mime make his silent world seem full of sound?

First we must remember that, for the mime, words are really no different from chairs. *They are all objects.* A chair is "made visible" through the way a mime moves and shapes his body around the invisible chair. And much the same is true for the mime and words. He makes us see the process of language. He hears, and we know there are words to hear. He sees a speaker, and we know there is a speaker to see. He feels the conversation; and, by turns, he is happy or sad, passionate or weak. When it is his turn to speak, his body fits around the language. He stands first one way and then another, first proudly, then romantically, or stupidly. His hands speak; his face talks. Of course, each word does not have to be made "visible." It is the "concept" of words that must be mimed, not individual meanings. If we had to make each word understood (by the movement of the lips), we would be better off speaking out loud. Miming a talk, a conversation? Of course! Mouthing words without sound? Nonsense!

95

Exercises for the Push

IN PUSHING, we move an object away from ourselves—away from the source of energy. In these exercises we are going to consider the most common kind of push, the hand push; and since hands can be positioned at various levels of the body, we will study different kinds of hand pushes according to the part of the body that serves as the energy source.

CHEST LEVEL 1. Positioning. The chest is thrust forward in anticipation of the effort to be invested, hands touching the object. (50)

2. Clic, Resistance, and Compensation. This movement is the actual push and must be done continuously. Both the chest and arms contract, releasing the energy in the clic. At the same time, the

54

hands move forward, resisting their own movement. (51)

While the hands are moving forward, the chest moves backward in order to compensate and to emphasize the conflict between the energy of the body and the mass of the imaginary object being pushed. The total image will be one of great strain and effort.

TORSO LEVEL 1. Positioning. The torso is forward and the hands are on the object. (52)

2. Clic, Resistance, and Compensation. The clic and resistance are the same as shown in the push from the chest (53). In this case, the torso moves backward for compensation during the push. (54)

97

HIP LEVEL 1. Positioning. The hips are forward; hands touch the object. (55)

2. Clic, Resistance, and Compensation. Again the clic and resistance are the same as in the push from the chest; here the hips move backward in compensation. (56)

In all three of these push exercises (chest, torso, and hips), the clic must be done as a rapid contraction of all the directly involved parts. Clearly, the hands, as the immediate contact of energy with mass, must clic sharply and distinctly. But it is especially important for the source of energy itself (chest, torso, *or* hips) to clic; the clic at each of these levels gives substance to the movement and emphasis to the energy. If the push

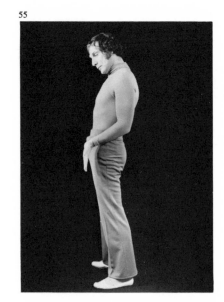

55

56

57

is successful and imaginary object is meant to move, body compensation is not total. (57) Only against an immovable object does one use complete compensation.

AN UNSUCCESSFUL PUSH, one that is unable to displace an object, is done in the following way:

1. Positioning. The torso is forward (but of course this could be done in a chest-level or hip-level position); hands touch the object.

2. Clic, Resistance, and Compensation. The torso moves backward and the arms extend fully. But since the point of this movement is to indicate an unsuccessful push, the hands must stay on the same spot in space. Therefore, compensating totally, one takes one step

backward to neutralize the effect of moving the arms forward.

An unsuccessful push can also be reduced to the clic only, dispensing with compensation. This is, in fact, a common form of the unsuccessful push. Once one realizes that something won't budge, one often gives up.

So far all the pushes looked at are those in which the body faces the object to be moved, certainly the most frequently used and most efficient kind of push. Yet there are variations: the side push, the back push, as well as pushes from virtually any angle of the compass. The technique for these is the same as for the forward push; only the direction of the push varies, followed by appropriate variations in the direction of the compensation.

IN THE UP PUSH AND THE DOWN PUSH, a special problem arises. How does one compensate? Since both of these pushes move on a vertical plane, how does one compensate vertically with the chest, torso, or hips? The solution is to continue to use a horizontal form of compensation. The up push is treated as though we were pushing an object ahead of us; the down push, as though the object were behind us. (58,59) Therefore, in the up push, we compensate by moving the chest, torso, or hips backward as we did in the chest-level push; in the down push, we compensate by moving the central part forward. (60,61)

58

59

60

61

62

63

64

PULLING consists in moving an object toward the source of energy within the body that is initiating the pull. Normally, it is done with the hands grabbing the object from the waist level since this is the most efficient; the center of the body provides the best counterweight and the best leverage.

THE SIDE PULL 1. Positioning. The hands reach out to grab the object; at the same time, the body is bent away from the hands. (62)

2. Clic, Resistance, and Compensation. At the clic, draw the hands back toward the waist; simultaneously move the body, particularly the waist and hips, forward toward the object being pulled. The energy initiates in the hips. Clic and resistance are felt in both the arms and the hips. (63)

The mime uses the side pull most frequently since it is most easily understood by the audience; it is quickly "read" at a distance. Other pulls can be used and each follows exactly the same principles as the side pull. The most common of the waist-level pulls are the front pull and the combined front-side pull. (64)

101

THERE ARE TWO VERTICAL PULLS, the up pull and the down pull. As we have seen in the up push and the down push, one cannot compensate vertically. For this reason, vertical compensation is once again identified with horizontal compensation. In the up pull, the source of energy is the chest; it compensates by moving toward the object being pulled. In the down pull, the source of energy is the hips, and they compensate by moving forward also.

65

66

THE UP PULL 1. Positioning. Hands reach up to take; the chest is back. (65)

2. Clic, Resistance, and Compensation. At the clic, the hands pull down close to the chest, while the chest thrusts forward. (66)

THE DOWN PULL 1. Positioning. Hands are down to grab; the body is bent; and the hips are away from the hands. (67)

2. Clic, Resistance, and Compensation. As the hands pull up toward the waist, the hips move forward. This brings the energy of the body and the mass of the object together in a shared center of gravity close to the hands. (68)

Many variations of the up pull and down pull are possible. Most variations consist of greater involvement of the legs. Common examples are ringing the bell, pulling from a well, or climbing a rope. (69)

ONCE HAVING MASTERED the push and the pull and the subordinate skills of clic, touch, resistance, manipulation, and compensation, you should be able to move any object, large or small. From the principles of the two basic acts, push and pull, you will be able to run through a wide range of actions, from the quite extreme to the very subtle, from the somewhat

heroic to the more prosaic. You may exhibit your strength by bending a rigid iron bar, or you may stretch a bow and shoot an arrow. If you like, you may simply wring out your laundry.

The exercises in this section, as well as those to come, are not to be taken as being definitive; they represent the essential structure for positions and movements. Try each one at a different angle; the effect will change: instead of wringing laundry, you will be wringing someone's neck.

The compass has 360 degrees, so does your body; in most cases, the exercises have shown you only the primary quadrants, leaving you to experiment with the degrees in between. And you will also find that the combination of several exercises will create a quite expansive repertory of meaning.

After you have learned to orchestrate the clic, resistance, and compensation, you will begin to create your own natural rhythms. You will discover ways of giving actions a particular life and substance by adding to them your own idiosyncratic emphasis—a certain arch to your body, a bend, or a slight twist. These nuances will come only with practice and your own ease with the basic techniques. With this will come your own style, an element that only you can add to your performance.

5. The Subject as an Object
Reactions

We have learned to move objects, but we must not forget that there are times when we too are objects—when we are pushed, shoved, pulled, or moved. We seem, in fact, to be objects a great deal of the time in our modern civilization. Everything is done for us—or, perhaps more precisely, much is done *to* us— so we have less to do ourselves.

Rather than taking the subway, we are taken by it; it carries us along. ("Leave the driving to us," they say, and we do.) We sit in the train passively, attempting to remain stable and still, perhaps drifting off into a half-hypnotic stare. The train starts. We are jolted, bumped, jarred, and shaken. Despite ourselves, we are in the midst of a ballet-pantomime, complete with rhythmical motions, suspenseful imbalances, and occasionally a marionette collapse.

To react involuntarily to outside energy directed at oneself may seem easier than to act directly on the outside world. After all, what does one have to do when one is the object? You push me, and I stumble away, pushed

back by the force of your energy. But if I am to push you, I must first have some energy so that I may direct it at you.

For the mime, at least, being the involuntary reactor is more difficult and sometimes more important than being the voluntary actor. There is nothing pushing him, yet he must seem to be pushed. He must create the illusion of something out there.

By reacting, the mime enriches and fills in his space. To begin with, he is all that his audience can see. He is the source of energy. When he acts, he reinforces his own presence and still remains at the center. But when he reacts, he transfers energy to somewhere else on the stage. Instead of only one actor, the audience can see now many other actors, some human and some mechanical but each with its own

power and its own substance.

Before going into reaction exercises, let us recall some of the simple laws of gravity and leverage that affect us when we are pushed or pulled.

Stand in back of me and pull my feet out from under me; my feet fly back and I fall forward: I fall away from the direction of the pull. Now stand in front of me and pull my feet; they will go forward and I will fall back. In both cases, I fall away from the direction of the thrust of energy. (The same principle is true, of course, for the push.)

Let us look again at our subway ride. The train "pulls" out, the very first motion causes us to fall opposite to the train's direction. For every pull there is a fall away from the direction of the pull. And for every push there is a fall away from the direction

of the push. This principle is true not only for our body as a whole but for its segments.

In simplified terms, the point at which the energy makes contact with the body establishes the base on which the reaction takes place. In the example we used of being pulled, the energy was directed to the feet; here the base of the reaction was the same as the base of the body. The rest of the body reacted by going in a direction opposite to that of the energy.

If the energy is applied at the waist, the reaction starts at the waist and moves upward to the head, primarily taking in the upper part of the body. One must also consider the magnitude of the force; the amount of force delivered will define the amount of reaction.

Cartoons

Cartoons have long realized the value of the basic elements of Mime technique. With a fantastic flair and instinct for the physical expression, cartoon makers have materialized fantasy.

Popeye, Bugs Bunny, Mickey Mouse, the Road Runner, and dozens of other creations might well have been the result of a mime's imagination. The mime and the cartoonist approach constructing realities in much the same ways, with many of the same limits and many of the same freedoms.

Both start with an empty space that is free to be filled in by visual details. Sound is not an important element in most cartoons and certainly is not for the mime. The cartoonist's freedom allows him to be surreal when it suits his imagination. Pieces of action can be followed quite literally to their absurd conclusions, or they can be bent and twisted into new directions. To some extent, this is what the mime can do; he can bend and reshape events and their logic.

There is also much similarity in the way the principles of pressure and tendency and manipulation are used in Mime and in cartoons. The mime uses pressure, and the cartoonist draws a character with an enormously puffed-up chest. Both expose the ridiculousness of the braggart. The mime creates a forward tendency; the cartoonist gives his character an exaggerated forward tilt. Both portray a threatening gesture. A safe falls on a cartoon character's head and his head continues to vibrate. A mime, on the other hand, vibrates his head to indicate that some invisible object has hit it.

Cartoons can always go one better than Mime, for there are limits to what the mime can do. The cartoonist can materialize literary figures of speech, making metaphors into realities. We see his characters puffed with pride, eyes shooting flames, figures red with rage, mad with joy, full of inclinations, or spitting fire. The mime cannot do all of that; he can only look on with some awe at an art that can.

107

Exercises for Reactions

CHEST-LEVEL PUSH 1. If one is being pushed forward, the pressure, of course, has been applied at the back. The chest thrusts forward as the head falls backward, because the head in this case is the first segment above the base of the reaction. After the reaction, body returns to its original position. (70)

2. In a push backward, the pressure is applied at the front. The chest caves in as the head falls forward; then the body returns to the upright position. (71)

3. In the side push, the pressure is applied on one side. The chest moves away from the pressure as the head falls sideways toward the source of the push. Once again, after the reaction, the body returns to its original position. (72)

In all of these exercises, the motions of both the chest and the head are combined so that they are virtually simultaneous; there is, however, an instant of delay in the fall of the head since it should ap-pear *as the result* of the sudden movement of the chest. You will also discover that once the reacting segment has moved, there is sometimes a momentum. Instead of returning to the upright position immediately, the rest of the body will follow along. Momentum will be especially important if the push has been relatively strong. To realize it, take a step that follows the direction of the push but only after the primary reaction has been presented.

THE HIP-LEVEL PUSH is more complicated than the chest push because there are two segments above the base of the reaction instead of one. There is the head and there is the torso. Since a push at the hips involves these two separate segments, each will react in its turn, creating the effect of a whip, quite similar to undulation. Energy is transmitted upward; the motion initiated in one segment is transferred to the next.

Assume, for instance, that one is

108

71

72

kicked in the rear end. There are two possible reactions. The first one simply follows the basic principles already considered. Everything above the hips—that is, the torso and head—will fall in one sudden back bend. In the second reaction, the whip effect is brought into play. The forward thrust of the hips is transmitted to the torso; the torso then thrusts forward and only then does the head fall backward. This second kind of push is called the whip instead of the fall because the head, in this case, does a double, up-down motion.

The first reaction in which the body bends is the reaction of a stiff body. The second reaction in which the upper body undulates slightly is the reaction of a supple, relaxed body. The undulating-whip reaction is in many ways a more forceful movement since it takes more time and space; the audience has more opportunity to absorb what is happening, as though it were all taking place in slow motion. (See undulation, page 54.)

109

THE WHIP 1. Pushed forward, from in back, the hips thrust forward, followed by the torso, as the head whips backward in a one-two rhythm. (73)

2. Pushed from the side, the hips thrust sideways, followed by the torso, as the head whips to the other side closest to the push. (74)

3. Pushed backward, from in front, the hips thrust backward, followed by the torso, as the head whips forward. (75)

THE PULL. We can be pulled from many directions and at different parts of the body. The most common pull is the one that engages both our hands and our arms, when we are tugging at a rope and whatever is at the other end pulls back. The tug of war is a good example of this. (See the flip sequence.)

There is also the waist-level pull in which an imaginary rope is tied around our middle and we are

73

74

110

dragged off. The technique for these pulls follows the same principles as those for the push. We must remember only that the pull is a reversed push. Standing in front of someone and pushing is the same thing as standing in back of him and pulling. The energy force is moving in the same direction; in reacting, the body falls away from the direction of the thrust of this energy.

In these exercises, we shall practice only the arm pull since the variations can be easily worked out.

1. In being pulled forward by the arms and hands, the hands have already grabbed something (a rope, for instance) or are attached to something. The hands, arms, and shoulders thrust forward as the head falls back. (76)

2. In the backward pull, the hands, arms, and shoulders thrust backward as head falls forward. (77)

111

3. In the sideways pull, the hands, arms, and shoulders thrust toward the source of the pull, while the head falls away from the pull to the other side. (78)

4. Try limiting these exercises by working only with the shoulders as though an invisible hand had suddenly grabbed one. The sense of surprise can be most effective. (79)

5. Combinations using both the pull and the push are possible. In one you might imagine walking a dog. The dog pulls on his leash; you react to the various angles and tensions he creates as he tries to get away. At the same time, you will be pulling him, which will be similar to being pushed from in front. Try passing the leash from one hand to the other. You may also combine pulling and being pulled by creating a ferocious tug of war; this will exemplify both action and reaction.

78

79
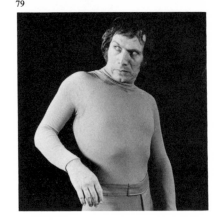

Walks and Runs

Imitation

Miming is not the same thing as imitating, although the ability to imitate is a rich resource of the mime. Imitation by itself is far too restricting. We can learn by imitating because it shows us how to behave. But imitation always shows us what has been or is; it cannot show us what might be. So a mime who rests his skill on the ability to imitate freezes his art because he freezes the reality that he can explore and create. Of course, the mime should use and develop his capacity to imitate—or else how will he be able to identify with the world outside himself, becoming a plant, an animal, some object, or even another person?—but he will have to know how to do more if he is to create a living and credible reality.

LOCOMOTION. After a certain age, getting around on our feet becomes second nature. After we get beyond crawling, we progress quickly through walking, to running, to climbing. Unlike reactions, these forms of movement are for the most part voluntary kinds of displacement. Gravity being what it is, we instinctively take to slipping and sliding, although a controlled slip or slide is harder to manage, as anyone knows who has tried to learn how to ice-skate or roller-skate.

Once having learned to move about, why does the student of Mime have to learn how to do it all over again? Aside from the fact that he has no staircase so he must learn how to walk up and down an imaginary one, his stage is as firm as the ground he usually walks on.

He must relearn walking and running because the illusion he is creating has very little to do with the ground he is on but a

great deal to do with the space he is in. If he walks normally, he will quickly disappear into the wings. He needs to learn how to push aside the limits of the real space he is using. He needs to know how to change its value so that in the space of a few yards he may walk from one end of a main street to the other.

This is the reason for learning how to walk or run on the spot; it allows the mime to make the space move around him as he remains virtually stationary. This walk gives the illusion of the ground moving under him, as though it were a vaudeville treadmill.

By extension, it can appear that the entire environment is moving too. If he uses his eyes to make contact with the "new" objects he comes upon, the walk on the spot can create a quite effective illusion. Sometimes, of course, a real walk in real space will be necessary; there will be nothing wrong in doing one. The

mime should not disregard what he already knows for the new things he learns. He must remember to put them together.

THERE ARE TWO KINDS OF WALKS: the pressure walk and the profile walk. Depending upon what you are doing and the style you wish to do it with, you will select one walk over the other. The profile walk is the classic walk of the mime. If you have seen Jean-Louis Barrault miming a walk in *Children of Paradise,* you will have seen him using the profile walk. As its name suggests, it is best done in profile so the audience can have a side view of the legs. Because of this view, the movement of the legs is emphasized, making the walk highly stylized and giving it a particular formalized grace.

This walk enhances the illusion of walking some distance along a linear plane. Since there

114

is no vanishing point that the audience can see, the mime appears to be walking into a space without limits. Scenes run parallel to him on either hand, but there is no clear end in sight. The mime can come to the end of this walk only by stopping. As you might suspect, its highly stylized qualities present important restrictions. It is almost impossible to change direction when using it, and it does not allow one to move easily into other kinds of action.

Its companion run, the profile run, creates at best only half an illusion, depending—as you will see in the discussion of it—upon the audience agreeing to a strict convention. As will also be apparent when we take up the mechanics of this walk, it does not seem to press against anything. In fact, an equally accurate name for this walk could be the vacuum walk. It is hard to use the profile, or vacuum, walk to mime walking against the wind or

pushing one's way through a crowded and bustling world, for the very character of this walk is to create an empty track along which the mime moves.

The pressure walk is a walk for all seasons. It is highly suited for a casual stroll in place, although it can be used for more emphatic strides. Its virtue is that it is quite flexible and versatile. It allows one to change direction without losing efficiency, and the pressure run flows naturally out of it. Because of its mechanics, it seems to push against surfaces, therefore combining well with other actions and reactions. (As we shall see, it can be used when walking against the wind, page 130.)

I start the exercises for both these walks with the one for the pressure walk since I find it the most useful and the most fundamental. What limits there are to the profile walk will become apparent once the pressure walk has been understood.

Exercises for Walks and Runs

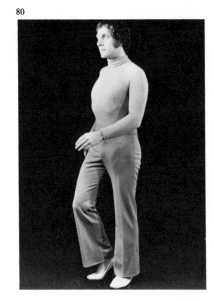

THE FORWARD PRESSURE WALK 1. Position Before the Walk. The body is straight, and the toes are slightly apart, with the heels together.

2. Step. The "stepping" foot is raised so that the toes are down and the heel is up. The knee of this leg is bent—this keeps the height of the body the same during the movement. (80)

3. Pressure. The "stepping" foot presses down. As the heel touches the ground and the knee straightens, the other foot backs away. This is the crucial part of the movement. Imagine that you are standing on a thin cushion of air. As the heel comes down, it produces pressure as if the air underfoot were being squirted away. As the cushion is pressed, the other foot is blown away, or "chased" away. (81)

When the other foot moves back, it stays *parallel to the ground* at all times, while the leg remains straight. By keeping the foot parallel and the leg straight, one achieves the effect of the ground running under the feet. This foot should not move back more than twelve inches so as not to force it out of its parallel position; a good average is six inches, although for a mincing walk one might use less, and for a bolder stride, more.

The balance of the body is *always* on the "stepping" foot. This balance allows the "chased" foot to be slightly above the floor and thus to glide back. The movement to this point completes half the walk. (It may be helpful to practice this walk divided in half. First try half the walk, using one foot as the "stepping" foot, then the other as the "stepping" foot.)

4. The Return. The "chased" foot is brought forward to its original position. At the beginning of the return, the leg of this foot will bend at the knee. When it reaches its

116

forward position, the foot steps down on the toes. This foot is now the "stepping" foot and is ready to chase the other.

DEPENDING UPON THE MOOD you wish to create, you will find different ways to use your arms. Most often you will want to let them follow the natural rhythm: the right arm moves with the left leg and the left arm moves with the right leg. This will be true for the profile walk and the runs.

In the pressure walk, we have thus far returned the "chased" foot to its original position, next to the first "stepping" foot. However, by varying the return, we can create some interesting illusions. If the returning foot steps down in front of its original position, the body moves slightly forward while appearing to walk in place. This creates a zoom-in effect. The whole scene moves closer to the audience since the mime *is* moving by slow increments toward the audience;

but because the relative relationship the mime has to his environment remains the same, the audience feels as though *it* is being moved in closer to the scene.

The zoom-out effect can be produced by returning the foot slightly in back of its original position. The audience then sees the scene as though from on a train moving away.

By returning the foot slightly to the side of its original position, we obtain a panning effect; the audience gets a panoramic view of the action as though it were moving across the action to take it in from a different angle. In all of these variations, the audience still believes it is watching a forward walk. From its point of view, only the angle or distance has been changed. The audience has been made into a camera that can zoom in, zoom out, or pan.

117

THE BACKWARD PRESSURE WALK is an uncomplicated modification of the forward pressure walk.

1. Position Before the Walk. The same as for the forward pressure walk.

2. Step. This too is the same. (82)

3. Pressure. The principle is the same, but here the "chased" foot glides forward, not backward, and thus moves ahead of its original position during the glide. (83)

4. The Return. The "chased" foot returns to its original position, touching down with its toes.

THE FORWARD PROFILE WALK. The mechanics of the profile walk make an almost perfect contrast to those of the pressure walk. You were asked to think of the pressure walk as producing a flow of air on which the "chased" foot glided. In the profile walk, we reverse the metaphor as well as the technique: you must now feel as though you were creating a vacuum that sucks in one foot.

82

83

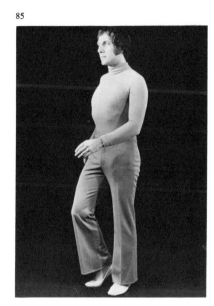

1. Position Before the Walk. The body is straight and the feet are together.

2. Step. The "stepping" foot takes a normal step forward. The foot comes down flat on the ground as the leg straightens. (The average step can be more than six inches, the average step of the pressure walk.) The balance of the body remains on the other foot. (84)

3. The Vacuum. Once the "stepping" foot has taken its forward position, a set of simultaneous movements occurs. The other foot rises on its toes; the heel goes up, and the knee naturally bends. If one thinks of this foot as the plunger of a pump, in raising it one makes a vacuum. Therefore, as the heel is drawn up, the "stepping" foot is sucked back to its original position. (85)

4. The Cycle. The foot that has served as the plunger becomes the "stepping" foot. Since it is raised on its toes and its leg is bent, it is ready to step forward, as described in number 2.

119

THE BACKWARD PROFILE WALK is a simple variation of the forward profile walk.

1. Position Before the Walk. The same as for the forward profile walk.

2. Step. The "stepping" foot moves backward about six inches and comes down flat on the ground as the leg straightens. The balance of the body remains on the other foot. (86)

3. The Vacuum. The principle is the same, but here the "stepping" foot glides back to its original position as the "plunger" foot pumps it back. (87)

4. The Cycle. The "plunger" foot now becomes the "stepping" foot, ready to step backward.

THE PRESSURE RUN is an easy extension of the pressure walk. It is structured to stress the up-down motion that makes the run look like a series of jumps—the basic

86

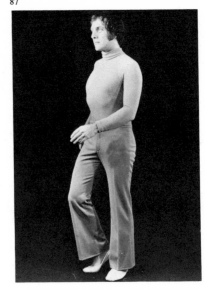

87

120

88

89

difference between walking and running in real life.

1. Position Before the Run. The body is straight, and the toes are slightly apart, with the heels together.

2. Step. Go up on both toes, keeping both legs straight. Balance your body on the "stepping" foot. (88)

3. Pressure. The "stepping" foot presses down. As the heel touches the ground, the knee continues to bend slightly. (This continuation of the knee bend is the major difference between the pressure run and the pressure walk.) As the heel touches down, the "chased" foot glides backward. The "chased" foot remains parallel to the ground, while its leg is straight. (89) (The pressure-and-glide principle here is the same as in the pressure walk.)

4. The Return. The body comes back to position 2. The balance is shifted to the newly returned "chased" foot, which is now ready to be the "stepping" foot.

121

THE PROFILE RUN is a simplification of the profile walk. It is done without the vacuum and operates according to a quite strict convention: only the leg nearest the audience steps; the hidden leg serves as a flexible pedestal for the action. The profile run is accepted by the audience not because it creates the illusion of a run but because it might be a run, given the context in which it appears and the strenuous motion it projects. Of course, it can only be done from the side.

1. Position Before the Run. The body is straight, and the feet are together.

2. Step. The supporting leg—the leg farthest from the audience—is straight, with the foot flat on the ground. The "stepping" leg moves forward; the knee and thigh rise to waist level and the toes of the foot point down. It should look somewhat like a strut held in mid-air. During this step, the upper body bends forward slightly. (90)

3. Flexion. Without touching the floor, the "stepping" foot makes a continuous motion through its original position. After it passes through its original position, it becomes parallel to the floor for its glide backward. Its rear position is above the ground at a distance from the body that allows it to remain comfortably parallel to the ground. During sweep of the "stepping" foot, the supporting leg flexes somewhat in order to provide spring to the movement. (91)

4. The Return. Once the "stepping" foot is at its rearmost extension, it immediately returns to position 2. At the instant of return, give the foot a sharp flip so that the toes will be pointing down during the rest of the return. During the return, the supporting leg will straighten. Since the supporting leg provides the bounce for this action, one can enhance the bounce by increasing the spring of the supporting leg. This will come naturally. You will find that you can raise the heel of the supporting leg during the flexion and even hop on the supporting foot. (92)

90

91

92

93

94

THE BICYCLE. The illusion of the bicycle can be developed as a variation of either the profile run or the pressure run.

1. Profile Variation. This requires no major change in the basic profile run, except that the movement of the leg must be "rounded off" to follow the circular motion of an imaginary pedal. The hands hold an imaginary handlebar, the upper torso is slightly bent over the bar, and the supporting leg provides a spring action as in the profile run. (93)

2. Pressure Variation. This is much like the basic pressure run except that the foot is *not* "chased" away. Keep both toes continually on the ground, moving from one foot to the other. Remember that you must go up high on your toes as though you were doing the pressure run. (94)

Mime as a Form of Philosophy

[The pantomime's] performance is as much an intellectual as a physical exercise: there is meaning in his movements; every gesture has its significance; and therein lies his chief excellence. The enlightened Lesbonax of Mytilene called pantomimes "manual philosophers," and used to frequent the theater, in the conviction he came out of it a better man than he went in. And Timocrates, his teacher, after accidentally witnessing a pantomimic performance, exclaimed: "How much have I lost by my scrupulous devotion to philosophy!" I know not what truth there may be in Plato's analysis of the soul into the three elements of spirit, appetite, and reason: but each of the three is admirably illustrated by the pantomime; he shows us every passion under the control of reason; this last—like touch among the senses—is all-pervading. . . . I have heard someone hazard a remark to the effect that the philosophy of Pantomime went still further, and that in the *silence* of the characters a Pythagorean doctrine was shadowed forth.

Lucian, *Of Pantomime*
(second century A.D.)

124

Climbs

Thus far we have concentrated on horizontal movement. Walking or running, when done well, can certainly be impressive; but it does use the well-established plane of the stage. All things being equal, the audience is ready to believe that the mime is able to move along the surface of the stage—even if he "moves" by staying in one place. Climbs, or steps up and steps down, open up another dimension; and by doing them correctly the mime can move into a three-dimensional world. He can now present hills and valleys, buildings and cities. Without these two steps, it will be hard for the mime to look down on the world he has made or to make clear that there is a reality above him that can be reached.

The step up transmits a sense of energy and of expanded effort. The mime pushes against gravity, against his own weight, in addition to pushing against the real floor, in order to lift himself to another level. The step down must appear as a drop into gravity. Therefore it should seem to take less energy, although to do it takes no less of the mime's real energy than the step up.

The mime walks up and down stairs in a manner somewhere between that of a baby and that of an adult: The baby discovers something new in each step; the adult takes it all for granted. The mime knows what he is doing, but he must still take one step at a time. If he does not, his audience will lose sight of the sharp progression up or down.

To produce the effect of a steep ascent or descent, like going up or down a ladder, the steps should be done on the spot, in the spirit of the spot walks. Both the step up and the step down are best done in profile, although they can be done in combination with turns to make a spiral staircase.

Exercises for the Climbs

STEPPING UP 1. Position Before the Step Up. The body is straight, and the feet are loosely together.

2. The Mark. Raise the "stepping" foot an average of six inches and then lower the foot to the ground, a few inches in front of its original position, toes down, heel up, and knee bent. Bend your body forward slightly as you make the mark. (This bend is necessary because in a normal step up, the angle between the "stepping" leg and the torso diminishes.) (95)

3. Lift. With the heel of the "stepping" foot already raised, lift your body to full extension so that you are on the toes of both feet and legs and body are straight. (96)

4. Land. In a continuous motion flowing immediately out of the lift, drop the "stepping" heel and bend the knee of the other leg, leaving its heel up. (Be careful not to bend knee of the "stepping" leg.) (97)

95

96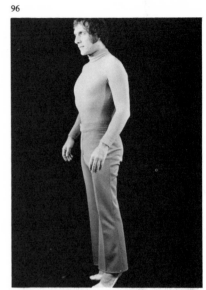

97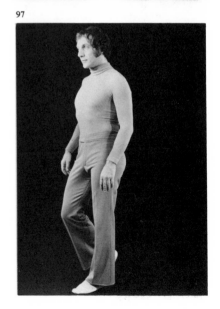

5. The Cycle. The bent leg is now ready to be the "stepping" leg and moves up to make the mark.

STEPPING DOWN. 1. Position Before the Step Down. The body is straight, and the feet are loosely together.

2. The Level. On one foot, raise the body as high as possible by rising on the toes; this leg is kept straight. The other foot will be off the ground and parallel to it; this non-supporting leg will also be straight. (98)

3. The Drop. In a continuous motion flowing immediately out of the level, drop the non-supporting foot flat to the ground, a few inches in front of its original position. As you drop this foot, bend the other leg at the knee with the heel still up. (99)

4. The Cycle. The leg that has just dropped will now raise the body by performing the level, position 2.

127

Exercises for the Climbs (cont.)

THE STAIRCASE. Mime becomes more persuasive when several movements are combined. This is true for walking up or down a staircase that has been given a railing. Hand manipulation adds the railing and thereby adds texture and highlight to the total movement.

1. Upstairs. The railing is a diagonal that runs along your side. As you make the mark with your foot, grab with a fully extended arm at about chin level. Then, during the lift and land, pull your hand down on a diagonal for about ten inches to indicate the distance covered by your body on its way up. Repeat the process for each new step. (100)

2. Downstairs. Start by grabbing the railing at around the hips with the arms fully extended; then pull the hand diagonally toward you about ten inches as you go through the level and land. You will find it more efficient to grab the banister at every other step. (101)

3. A Variation: Try keeping your hand on the railing during two or

100   101

even three up or down steps. One has to be careful to cover the same distance with the hand at each step and, also, to keep the shape of the railing.

Do not forget at the end of each pull to release the railing before going on to the next grab.

THE LADDER is very much like the staircase, except that it is done on a steep vertical and there are two railings to be grabbed instead of one. You may pull at the same time on the sides, or one hand after the other. You may also pull on the crossbars at the same time with both hands or one hand after the other, a different hand for each bar. Facing the ladder and walking down it is similar to the backward profile walk to which one adds an up-down motion. Don't forget to reverse the hand motion, and good luck.

128

Friction: Wind, Water, and Slide

Protean Man

If I am not mistaken, the Egyptian Proteus of ancient legend is no other than a dancer, whose mimetic skill enables him to adapt himself to every character: in the activity of his movements, he is liquid as water, rapid as fire; he is the raging lion, the savage panther, the trembling bough; he is what he will. The legend takes these data, and gives them a supernatural turn—for mimicry substituting metamorphosis. Our modern pantomimes have the same gift, and Proteus himself sometimes appears as the subject of their rapid transformations.

Lucian, *Of Pantomime*
(second century A.D.)

The mime lives with three elements: air, water, and earth. He does not have to concern himself directly with fire; it is a bit too mystical even for the mime, although a walk through fire might be a rather interesting effect!

Air, water, and earth are the elements he must struggle with. Each provides a certain texture and richness to his empty stage. He can create a windy day by using the illusion of weight and pressure; his audience can see the wind, if not feel it. He can step quite easily into water by moving into slow motion; the water will seem to restrain him and it will buoy him up too. For want of something so simple as friction, he will alter his relationships with the ground. A slip or a slide and he will rediscover the earth.

The primary function of the exercises in this section will be to make your feet more intelligent. The only reality the mime touches is that under his feet, and the mime who speaks well with his feet will have come some way toward living in the reality of water, earth, and air.

129

Exercises for Friction

102

103

WALKING IN THE WIND 1. The Advance. Start with a pressure walk. As you wish the wind to take hold, accentuate the pressure in your walk and bend your torso backward. (The torso gets the main thrust of the wind since it is the most solid surface of the body and the most exposed.) (102)

2. The Recoil. After the pressure on the torso becomes too great, it gives in to the wind and caves in. You will be pushed back. You should move back in a series of small, rapid steps, very much like the effect of the zoom-out in the pressure walk. (103)

3. The Cycle. Build back to the advance with slow, determined steps and a slow increase of the bend in your torso. Vary the pressure and rhythm as much as possible in order to capture the sudden unpredictability of wind bursts. You will find a natural pattern for your hands as they participate in the struggle.

WALKING INTO WATER. In this exercise, we shall assume that the water becomes progressively deeper, moving from ankle depth all the way to total immersion. To warm up, turn back to the resistance exercise for the foot (page 82). Put one foot at a time into the water. Move each foot from side to side, flipping at each change of direction. (Remember the flip is accompanied with a clic, followed by resistance.) Having thus tested the water, we are now ready for the walk.

1. Ankle Level. The step is the same as the pressure walk in which the "stepping" foot "chases" the other away. Use a normal pressure-walk return, but flip the foot with a clic at the beginning of the return and follow with a resisted movement in order to show the slowing effect of the water. (The point of clic registers the level of the water. It will move up as the level of the water moves up the body.) (104)

2. Knee Level. Again the step is the same as the pressure walk, but the "chased" foot glides back more slowly and reaches farther back. In the return, the knee clics and resists. The foot will not clic now, but it will still be pointing down on the return. (105)

104

105

131

3. Hip Level. The step is the same as for the knee-level walk. On the return, the hip on the side of the "chased" leg clics with a little thrust forward that punctuates the forward motion of the leg. The forward motion of the "chased" leg is slow. There is a very mild bend in the knee and the toes are pointing down as leg comes back to the stepping position. (106)

4. Waist Level and Above. At this point, so much of the body is immersed that we need think only of the principle of buoyancy: the water supports enough of our body so we float. All the parts of our body in the water move in slow motion, with the feet indicating the upward push of the water by a constant up-down motion. Dance on the balls of your feet, together or alternatively. When you are sufficiently immersed in the water, the hands can start to take part, similar to the movement in the resistance exercise for hands. (See page 82.) If we want, we can start swimming by using one leg as a pedestal. (107)

106

107

SLIDES. There are two basic kinds of slide. The first slide emphasizes one foot at a time—one foot slides while the other is motionless. This kind of slide is quite necessary for many reaction movements. For example, in the tug of war, as you are being pulled, you will slip in the direction of the pull—one foot dragged and twitched across the ground while the other foot scissors up in the air to gain balance.

There is also Charlie Chaplin's famous use of the one-foot slide.

Coming to a corner at great speed, he loses traction; one foot skates around the corner while the other foot struggles in mid-air. By rhythmically swinging from one foot to the other, the one-foot slide can be turned into a quite convincing skating illusion.

The second kind of basic slide produces an effect very much like that of the ascent, descent, or pivot: the lower part of the body is isolated from the upper part. It looks as though the body is being

moved by some mechanical system, like a figure in a shooting gallery or the figure that pops out of a clock when it strikes the hour.

1. Sliding on One Foot. The simplest way to do this is to stand on both feet, first sliding one foot away and back and then repeating the action with the other foot. Balance yourself on the motionless foot, and then slide the other foot away, using a toe-heel motion that will make the foot zigzag across the floor. (108)

A more interesting one-foot slide requires that you stand on the foot that you are sliding away. Be careful to allow the zigzag to twist your leg only up to the hip; the rest of your body will lean in the direction of the slide. Your other leg is off the ground. After sliding a few inches in one direction, drop back on the other foot and repeat the movement in the other direction.

By doing this slide in one direction only, you can create Chaplin's corner turn or highlight the effect of being pulled in the tug of war. (See the tug-of-war flip sequence.) By developing a rhythmical exchange between feet and adding a swing of the body and arms, you can create the illusion of ice-skating. (109)

2. Sliding on Two Feet. Start with the heels together and the toes apart; then slide the toes together, moving the heels apart. Of course, you may move in either direction. By adding some intermediate positions of the feet, you can slide forward.

First, place both feet together. Second, slide the heels apart, keeping the toes touching. Third, slide the toes apart so that the feet are parallel but separated by about twelve inches. Fourth, slide the heels together, keeping the toes apart. Fifth, bring the toes together so that the feet are once more touching. Using this technique, you will inch forward. By reversing the positions, you may slide backward.

Part Three: Creating a World

6. The Mime of the Subject

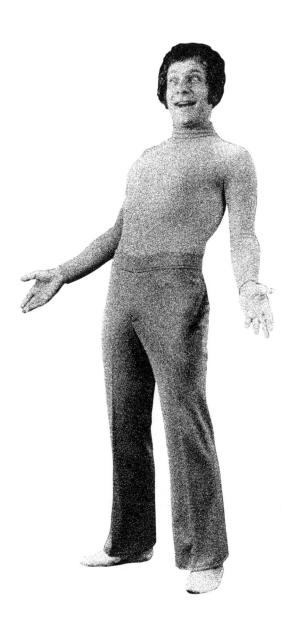

Let us begin with emotions. Often we feel before we know. A muscle tightens here; a shudder runs through us there; our back stiffens; or our stomach churns. I feel, therefore I am. At least I know I am present. (Is knowledge a rationalization of one's gut instincts? Perhaps.)

Whatever the emotion is—anger, hysteria, tenderness, or joy —each one begins by announcing itself inside our body. Once established there, it surfaces. It seeps out through our pores; it reorders the structure of our posture; it changes the rhythm of our gait and the texture of our skin. To the shrewd observer, we are perhaps all but transparent.

The mime searches for ways to make the internal play of emotions apparent from the outside so that his audience can see that the character he presents is a man of feelings. The emotions the mime constructs and projects must fit his character well; they cannot simply be stapled onto the outside of his character like so many paper figures on a Halloween costume. They need to

137

spring from the center of the character, hence from the center of the mime's performance and movements.

In the Mime of the Subject, we consider how to make this connection between the inner world of feeling and the performance world of surface. It will be necessary to learn how to make physical something that is as ephemeral as spirit or soul or mood. Emotions are to be translated into motions; for although we begin with emotions, in Mime we must always end with movement.

What are some of the techniques the mime has at his disposal? They are quite simple and quite basic. It is their combination with each other and with the exercises of movement that makes a performance complex and a character deep and allows us to project motivation and nuance. But let us start by looking at these techniques in their basic form. Sometimes, for instance, the body seems to shrink or expand. At one moment we look small, terribly small, and

A Curriculum for a Mime

To arrive at a Perfection in this Art . . . a Man must borrow Assistance from all the other sciences (*viz.*) Music, Arithmetic, Geometry, and particularly from Philosophy, both Natural and Moral: He must also be acquainted with Rhetoric, as far as it relates to Manners and Passions; nor ought this Art to be a Stranger to Painting and Sculpture. . . .

Our Pantomime therefore ought to be well versed in History and Fable: His Knowledge should begin from the Chaos or Birth of the World; let him particularly learn the Division of Heaven and all the Celestial Fables: He should be well acquainted with the whole Attic Fable and the Records of Athens; next let him learn what is to be found worth his Observation in Corinth, and all the Stories in the Records of Nemea. He may also gather abundance of Examples from Lacedemon, Elis, Arcadia, and Crete. . . . He must be also well read in all the *Metamorphosis,* and must be admitted into the most secret Mysteries of the Egyptians: Our Pantomime also must not be unacquainted with the various Fictions of the Poetical Hell: And to sum up all in one Word, he must be ignorant of nothing which is to be found in Homer and Hesiod, and other eminent Poets, especially those who have wrote Tragedy, and must understand them perfectly and fully, and be ready to produce them into Action on Occasion.

John Weaver, *A History of Mimes and Pantomimes* (London, 1728)

we feel that way too; at another moment we feel like giants, and we puff up and swagger as we walk. This is *pressure* at work transforming us.

"I love you," I say and draw toward you. This is *tendency;* the body moves toward the source of its attraction. Or, "I love you," I say and back away. This too is tendency; the body expresses ambivalence, maybe timidity, maybe even dislike. In both instances, the direction in which the body leans helps to define the nature of an emotion and its relationship to an external world.

A third technique is *tension.* Think here of the casual walk that stiffens when a corner is turned and we come face to face with the unexpected. The elasticity of our body changes; our skin seems to thicken and stretch at the same time. In this case, it is fear that has brought about this change, but any sudden alteration of our relationship with our environment can do the same.

Finally, there is the *rhythm*

and speed of our movements. We jerk forward; we slide back. Our hands cut the air with a sharp syncopation that has nothing to do with the balance of the rest of our body. The tempo of our acts reflects our feelings, sometimes reinforcing what we are doing, sometimes undermining it completely. We speak through our rhythms, and only the blind cannot hear.

Thus far, in the chapters on "The Mime of the Object" and "The Subject as an Object," you have learned how to move on the stage in order to create certain kinds of physical effects and objects; but if you can only go through the motions, you will not be doing enough. Your performance will lack bite. You must create a subject for your acts.

Knowing how to mime an object, you will know how to suggest real objects in the space around you. By learning how to mime the subject, you will learn to affirm the presence of character and mood. Although for the purposes of this discussion I have

139

kept separate these two different aspects of Mime, we should not make the mistake of keeping them indefinitely separated. One is overlaid upon the other. To the act of doing we now add the verb of being; and the performance becomes richer and truer. In Mime, we will fail to be present on stage when we cannot do. Equally, we will fail to do well when we cannot be present as a character.

In all things, character seems to be indispensable, and this is no less true for Mime. To make a character walk and not merely to move across a stage is the point of Mime, and of all theater, for that matter. Things being what they are, a mime has no choice, he must create a character. He cannot do very much else. A character is there, as soon as he walks onto the stage, because his own character is there —his style makes its own appearance.

Starting with your own style, it becomes a question of learning

Delsarte: A Theory of Gesture

François Delsarte was a phenomenon of the nineteenth century. First in his own voice and later through the voices of his disciples, he developed a theory of gesture and communication that achieved international recognition. Acclaim often leads to popularization and distortion, and this was true for Delsarte's ideas. By the end of the nineteenth century, one could find advertisements for Delsarte corsets, cosmetics, and even a Delsarte wooden leg. Perhaps because of this, much of what he said has been forgotten or treated with great suspicion over the last seventy years. Yet this is unfortunate; distortions aside, Delsarte's studies of gesture, non-verbal language, and the relationship of a performer to his audience are suggestive and lucid.

In talking about theater and performance, Delsarte and his disciples often sounded like sociologists or psychologists. They saw the entire theater as a complex matrix of signals and interactions in which both the performers and the audience developed and transmitted meaning. It is not clear that social scientists in the area of non-verbal communication and body language have even heard of Delsarte, but one can find similarity between recent research and Delsarte's work of almost a hundred years ago. The influence of Delsarte on modern dance is quite clear. Ted Shawn, himself a central figure in modern dance, credits Delsarte with providing the base for modern dance. (A valuable discussion of Delsarte's theory is Shawn's book *Every Little Movement*.) One also hears the echoes of Delsarte in contemporary theater. "A word does not start as a word," says Peter Brook in *The Empty Space,* "it is an end product which begins as an impulse, stimulated by attitude and behaviour which dictate the need for expression." There is in that an unmistakable Delsartean ring.

L'Abbé Delaumosne, a student of Delsarte, shows the approach Delsartean thought took toward the audience, an approach with interesting similarity to that of writers like Jacques Ellul who consider the questions of propaganda and public psychology. "An audience must not be supposed to resemble an individual. A man of the greatest intelligence, finding himself in an audience, is no longer himself. An audience is never intelligent; it is a multiple being, composed of sense and sentiment. The greater the numbers, the less intelligence has to do. To seek to act upon an individual by gesture would be absurd. The reverse is true with an audience; it is persuaded not by reasoning, but by gesture.

"There is here a current none can control. We applaud disagreeable things in spite of ourselves—things we should condemn, were they said to us in private. The audience is not composed of intellectual people, but of people with senses and hearts. . . . It is not ideas that move the masses; it is gestures. . . . The basis of this art is to make the auditors divine what we would have them feel.

"Every speaker may choose his own standpoint, but the essential law is to anticipate, to justify speech by gesture. Speech is the verifier of the fact expressed. The thing may be expressed before announcing its name."

References:

Delsarte System of Oratory, containing the complete works of l'Abbé Delaumosne, the complete works of Mme. Angelique Arnaud, all the literary remains of François Delsarte, and lectures, lessons, and articles by others (New York: Edgar S. Werner, 1893)

Shawn, Ted. *Every Little Movement: A Book About François Delsarte* (New York: Dance Horizons, 1963)

how to cultivate it by developing your skill with pressure, tendency, tension, and rhythm, so that one style can be turned into many styles and reflect many personalities and moods in addition to the basic one you take home at night. Take off your predispositions as though they were so many costumes, and begin again, starting at zero. This zero state I call, naturally enough, Disposition Zero. (It has for its complements Position Zero and Pressure Zero.)

Disposition Zero is a point of reference from which the mime moves to establish and construct a character. It is a neutral state of being that reveals nothing of his inner feelings; it announces no intentions, any more than it indicates any withdrawal. If it were welded into a character on stage, it would produce a rather autistic soul. For this reason, it is rarely used except as the basic skeleton on which the mime builds in order to create and present a character.

Pressure

When we considered pressure earlier, we thought about it primarily from the point of view of its ability to maintain the position of the body in real space. In addition, pressure, along with the clic, was seen as the technique by which we were able to effect the illusion of change, of both action and reaction. Rather than thinking now about pushing or pulling objects in an imaginary world, or being pushed or pulled by them, we are going to turn to the somewhat metaphoric push-and-pulls of the psychological world. The psychological pressures *on* us manifest themselves by pressures *in* us.

If we start at Pressure Zero and Disposition Zero, we may move into either a positive state of pressure or a negative one. Roughly speaking, Positive pressure bespeaks a state of exultation. The ego is bold. It fills out to take in more space; and the body in turn expands to claim more room, so that both body and ego together may proclaim themselves more freely. The ego says through the body, "I am

"Gesture is the direct agent of the heart. It is the first manifestation of feeling. It is the revealer of thought and the commentator upon speech."

—François Delsarte

142

here. See *me*." This is an adventurous moment of the spirit.

Negative pressure, on the other hand, is a state of withdrawal, induced by despair or sorrow or sadness. The body shrinks as the ego shrinks. There is less to see because there is more to hide and more to protect. Pain hurts; pain punctures. Like a needle, both psychological and physical pain can deflate us, in the way a balloon is deflated. At the pin prick, the body slowly empties; losing its pressure, it collapses. We move from sadness to melancholy to deep depression, until we are drained and in complete collapse.

It is well to think of pressure in terms of the center of the body; for, as we have seen in the discussion of the trunk, the center of the body registers emotions like love and fear as well as the more raw, physical energies of the body itself. For these reasons, the center of the body serves as an important point of reference for emotions.

By using the center as a point of reference, the mime provides himself with an approach to emotions that allows him to combine technical control with natural expression. It is necessary for his audience to see an emotion as though it is happening naturally from within his character, without conscious efforts. (Emotions, after all, often overwhelm us without the least preparation on our part.) At the same time, the mime is himself quite conscious of the means he is employing to construct the emotion; but by keeping the center in mind and relating the flow of pressure to it, the mime creates a physical continuity that can be translated into an emotional one.

When, for instance, an emotion expands out from the center, through the torso and chest to the neck and shoulders and into the head and arms, the totality of this expansion asserts the totality of the emotion. The emotion has been given an organic consistency. It avoids being seen as a series of theatrical gestures, where "theatrical" is all too often synonymous with "artificial" and "faked."

A smile that only flickers

across the face without being reinforced by the chest remains an abstraction, a rather wry and detached gesture. Similarly, a greeting of welcome that rests in the arms and does not take in the shoulders and torso will appear false and contrived. The same principle is true for Negative pressure; the contraction includes the whole body, if the depression is to appear massive.

A basic rule of thumb: an emotion will be proportionately greater as it includes more of the body. It will seem more valid as its energy is drawn from the center of the body, or as it is drawn back into the center.

Of course, you may not always wish to create a "valid" emotion; sometimes a shallow smile or a false quiver of pain is exactly what is called for. It then

will be important to sever the pathway between the center and the rest of the body. One may wish to start an emotion in the center and freeze it abruptly, not giving it time to spread. Or one may wish to locate it only in an extremity without letting it reach back to the center.

As with all uses of pressure, the clic is very important. A series of clics in the course of radiating or contracting pressure will punctuate and highlight an emotion. Because it focuses the pressure, it increases the sense of continuity. Taken together, pressure and clic enable an emotion to develop its own natural course through the body, providing the time and space for it to happen.

For a set of preliminary exercises, return to those for the bend. (Pages 52–53.) They will

help you get in touch with your center and give you a chance to practice orchestrating pressure and clics.

The ability to "talk" with one's back is a good example of how expressive pressure can be. Try miming the reading of a letter. The point of this exercise is to use only your back to communicate a wide range of negative and positive emotions. Assume that this imaginary letter has both good and bad news in it. Done well, you should be able to register, sentence by sentence, paragraph by paragraph, all the changes in tone and content you find as you read. You will find that no one need read the letter over your shoulder to know what it is telling you.

Tendency

Positive tendency.

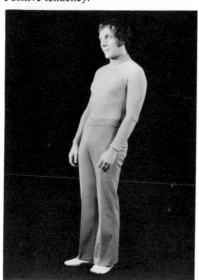

Negative tendency.

The body rarely stands perfectly straight, at zero. We each incline in one direction or another, forward or backward or to the side. While we may have a basic tilt that is characteristic to us, it will vary depending upon the circumstances, our mood, or the particular tempo of the moment. This tilt, or the tendency of the body to lean, complements pressure; the mime uses it to assert and clarify the force of a character's feelings.

Strictly speaking, inclination is the angle determined by the intersection of two planes. We can think of tendency as the intersection of emotional forces and emotional temptations. The lover leans forward, slowly and gently, drawing nearer his love; two planes of energy come together with one clear angle, one clear focus.

Often the intersection of emotional forces is not so straightforward; sometimes, in fact, instead of one angle with one focus, there are several angles, several focuses. For example, the lover who says "I love you"

145

while leaning backward is lost between two fields of force, his loved one and his own ambivalence. He is being pushed in one direction; he is being pulled in another. Tendency, then, is an emotional equivalent of push and pull, or of being pushed and being pulled.

Using zero as our point of reference, we have two basic kinds of tendency: positive tendency and negative tendency. Feelings like desire, courage, or aggressiveness tilt the body forward, indicating a readiness to move ahead; this is positive tendency. Fear, hesitation, or cowardice pulls the body back away from action, away from commitment; this is negative tendency.

In addition to these two basic inclinations, there is a side-to-side lean. A sway from one leg to the other, it is quite similar to the side-to-side tilt of the head. One is outside the action, on the sidelines. The body questions rather than hesitates. On the other hand, a forward-backward tilt emphasizes hesitation. The body faces a problem: to step into the action or to stand back from it. The side-to-side tilt bespeaks active neutrality; the forward-backward tilt presents active indecision.

For a series of preliminary exercises in tendency, return to those for the block (pages 56–57). Do the marionette, turning it into a creature of flesh and blood with, if not his sins, all of his tendencies.

To play out some of the uses of tendency, imagine the following scene, then mime it: One thinks that one recognizes a friend at a distance, only to discover as one comes closer that he is a stranger. To begin with, start by waving at him, then walk briskly toward him. This walk almost turns into a run, as the body tilts forward. But as there is less and less distance between you and your imagined friend, doubt sets in. Slow down and decrease the degree of your positive tendency until, ultimately, as it becomes clear that you have made a mistake, you draw back even as you drift forward. By the time you pass the stranger, your body should have taken a slight backward tilt of embarrassment and withdrawal.

In such situations, we avert our glance and remove ourself, as best as we can, in an attempt to erase our misplaced enthusiasm. The backward tilt is one of the ways we withdraw.

146

Combination of Pressure and Tendency
with a Touch of Tension

At heart, the mime is a Platonist. He renders a form of reality and tries to portray the essence of things. He either goes to the core of existing types, to see if there is more to discover, or he goes on to create new types. But he does not elaborate the uniqueness of a single personality; his search is most often for that which will not decay.

In this, he is unlike the actor, for the mime does not look for good characterization or the pyrotechnics of a good psychological presentation; either of these two would make his portrayal too particular or too special.

Nonetheless, he must be careful not to dissociate himself entirely from psychology and behavior. The too complete Platonist would mime only shadows; and, after all, the mime's vision is rooted in the complexity and irony of life itself, not in its reflections. So the mime's work must achieve a delicate balance. It must be spartan without being impoverished and psychologically rich without losing the universal meaning of its form.

Although I have isolated pressure from tendency for the sake of study, they can never be truly separated. Pressure gives us shape; tendency gives that shape direction. Together, they locate a character somewhere on a spectrum of emotions: he is sad *and* restrained, or he is buoyant *and* aggressive, or he is happy *and* timid. The combination multiplies emotional effects.

By relating one emotion to another, one enlarges the total emotional image; it becomes deeper and more complex. We can call this: giving the character an *attitude*. A position has been taken; the audience is now able to discern purpose. Once it can see purpose, it can see character, for the character has become a physically concrete expression of a psychological state.

Although one is able to project an attitude, one has not firmly fixed a character until one has added a certain amount of tension. You will recall that tension occurs just prior to movement. It is the moment in which the body prepares itself for what

147

it will do next, without doing it. For that reason, tension is an increment of nuance rather than a fact. It is an important nuance all the same, since it suggests what we can expect of the character.

In pointing the way to what he will do next, tension clarifies what he is doing and feeling now. Even more, it provides a dimension of psychological suspense, of human drama. I describe here something approaching a psychological freeze—a quite precise emotion hangs in the air, ready to be continued or to be transformed into another emotion.

This movement out of an attitude draws a continuum on which the character acts, one that allows us to see how it is he acts and how it is he might act. He is someone we can understand. What we are understanding is his behavior, and this behavior is nothing more than a collection of attitudes and the movement between them into new ones. Each new attitude has the power to expose a pattern of meaning and reality.

For some, pressing forward is a matter of leaning backward.

148

Behavior: Speed and Rhythm

While an attitude shows us how a character holds himself—what his position to the world and himself is at any instant in time—behavior shows us how he conducts himself. To know that is to know a good deal about who he is. What started as a frozen psychological image, a fixed point in space, has become a three-dimensional enactment.

Look carefully at someone who is sitting absolutely still. For all his immobility, you will see movements. These are not necessarily the movements of nervous energy; they are the expressions of internal rhythms—those internal processes of thinking and feeling that go on continually in everyone. The spirit dances inside the body and, in turn, the body picks up the rhythms. Every act and every gesture can be affected by the rhythm it is performed in. It reveals the nature of a character's control over himself, and therefore it reveals something of the quality of the inner spring that animates him.

There are many speeds for the same act, and each speed will change the weight of the act. The basic walk when judged from the point of view of its speed and rhythm is a complex thing. It is easy to walk, but it is not so easy to change or direct the tempo of your walk; this is true for most movements. Yet the meaning of the walk does change as its pacing changes. The gentle and graceful stroll can be altered into a slow and cautious tread by checking the tempo, or can be transformed into a jerky, flustered trot by accelerating the speed and movement of the body.

The speed with which we do things is not always apparent to us, although we are often aware of the speed of other people's movements. We all seem to operate according to our own metronome. It takes some effort to relate your own rhythms to those outside you. Frequently, there is a disparity, a time lag between the tempos. Sometimes the mime wants to take advantage of this disparity; it will allow him to separate his character from the world, creating a character who exists independent of the bustle around him.

149

Let us look, for instance, at how the French actor Jacques Tati uses this separation between tempos to construct the character of M. Hulot. Hulot is tall. He appears to be a normal man, with normal pressure and tension, except that his posture is a bit curious. His upper body, in particular, has a distinct forward tilt, emphasized by an upward and outward jut of his head. Simply by looking at him, we guess that he is ready to go ahead into the unknown—and that a good deal of the world about him, even the rather commonplace, is strange and new for him.

Much of the weight of his performance rests on the rhythm of his motions. It redirects and redefines his tendency. Completely erratic, with abrupt changes in speed and sudden transitions into new actions, Hulot bounces through the world. He is not the victim as much as he is the innocent, a

every one of the spectators identifies himself with the scene enacted, when each sees in the pantomime as in a mirror the reflection of his own conduct and feelings, then, and not till then, is his success complete. But let him reach that point, and the enthusiasm of the spectators becomes uncontrollable, every man pouring out his whole soul in admiration of the portraiture that reveals him to himself. Such a spectacle is no less than a fulfillment of the oracular injunction "Know Thyself"; men depart from it with increased knowledge; they have learned something that is to be sought after, something that should be eschewed.

But in Pantomime, as in rhetoric, there can be (to use a popular phrase) too much of a good thing; a man may exceed the proper bounds of imitation; what should be great may become monstrous, softness may be exaggerated into effeminacy, and the courage of a man into the ferocity of a beast.

Lucian, *Of Pantomime*
(second century A.D.)

Quixote, who can feel only his own logic and cannot see the logic of others. As is sometimes the case with people tensed to go ahead, Hulot often ends by going beyond.

In watching a performer like Tati, one becomes aware of how useful it can be to control one's rhythm and speed. To develop this control, you should practice a motion at a given speed, repeatedly, then very quickly, finally very slowly. After you have developed a rhythm, move through a progressive range of speed, accelerating and decelerating until you can perform the motion from the tempo of the hysterically rapid silent-movie chase to that of the slow-motion instant replay. (You may find it interesting to try varying tempo on some of the flip sequences in order to see how tempo relates to meaning. Change tempo only when the focus of the action changes, otherwise a change in tempo will have little meaning.)

151

Motivation and *Données*

Up to this point, we have considered *how to be* a character on the stage, but not yet *who to be*. This is clearly a more complex issue, with no pat set of answers. Learning how to use pressure or speed and rhythm well is far easier than learning how to be a fully rounded character, just as it is easier to learn how to walk or eat than to learn how to be a human being.

The mime does not have to begin at the beginning, though, when he starts to think about presenting a character. The techniques he has learned thus far equip him to construct the physical reality of a character; together, they put character virtually within his grasp.

Character is a combination of givens. You may start by stipulating a certain kind of character with a set of psychological values who comes from a specific social and historical background. For example, one may decide to create the role of a poor boy who is timid and lost. Once one understands this character, one may put him into situations— a candy store or a busy city street

Young Hood. *Men and Dreams.*

Mother Fox. *Renard.*

—and develop his reactions. This is an approach which starts with the inner motivations of character.

On the other hand, one may wish to start with a series of external motivations in order to develop a character. For example, think of a series of events or psychological states or physical contexts which you want to examine. Move through this context making a character to fit.

You may be interested in considering what it is like to work in an anonymous office in a busy, impersonal city. As you work through that space, you may discover that what you have to say demands that you use a young boy fresh from the country, or a middle-aged woman who has just left her husband and is trying to find a new life and a new career, or a tired executive who has been at his job for thirty years and is bored and blasé. So

much will depend upon what you want to say. And so much will depend upon how freely you can allow yourself to stumble into truths that make sense as you explore.

Don't make the mistake of assuming that you must start *either* with a clearly established character *or* with an external set of motivations. There should be a mixture of approaches. As you act, you will create things to react to, and those things will show you new things and suggest new actions. The ability to react creatively and imaginatively is a tool as important as any of the others you are learning. It is at this moment that object mime and subject mime come together. Above all, understand your own *données,* make them clear to yourself, and a character cannot help but emerge.

153

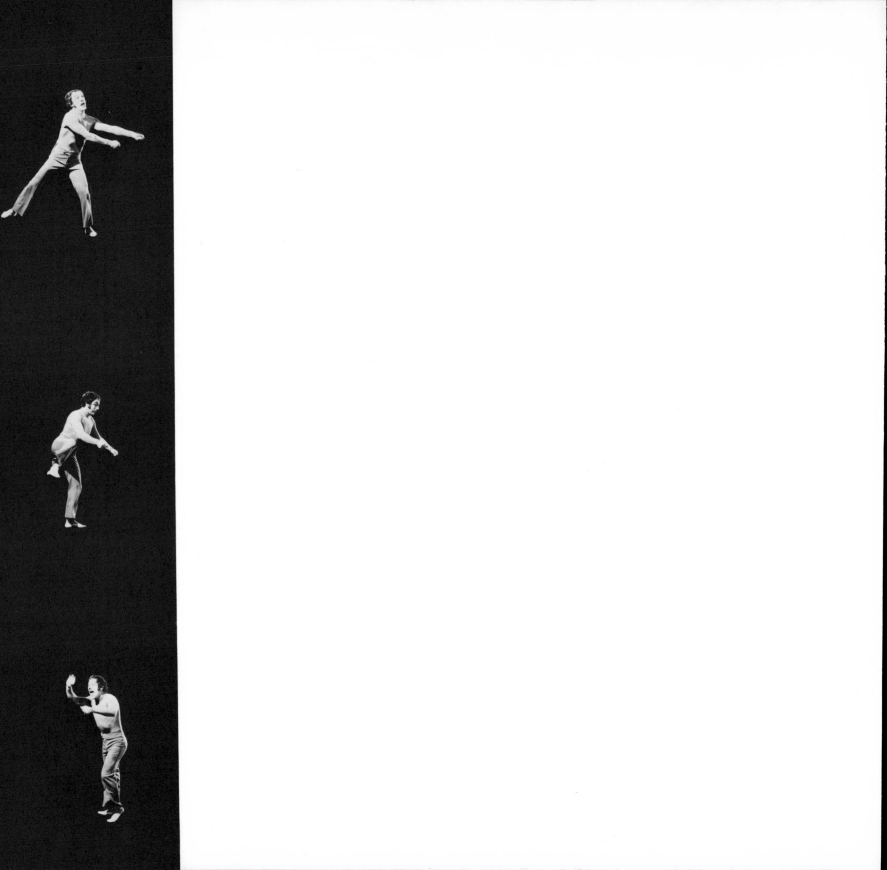

7. Pantomime

Once you have mastered the techniques of Mime, you will want to stage them in order to give shape and substance to a vision. Pantomime is such a composition of Mime techniques.

I can give you no easy formulas. You will have to learn how to feel your way along, taking characters and actions you feel comfortable with and putting them together so that they come close to saying something that means something to you.

You have already met some of the fundamental techniques of Mime illusion, and you now have the beginnings of how to project a credible character. In the next chapter, "The Uses of Imagination," we will talk about improvisation as a way of discovering what it is you want to say through Mime. In that light, the uses of style and form will become equally important as ways of clarifying and sharpening what you have to say.

For the present, though, we shall concern ourselves with three basic elements in the structure of a pantomime: the event, the situation, and the conflict.

The Triangle: The Mime, the Actor, the Dancer

Actors and dancers coexist rather pacifically because they have so little in common. Once the mime enters, discord follows. No one will give the poor fellow room. The actor wants to claim the mime's speaking body, and the dancer claims his silent movements. It seems that many people will not let a mime be a mime. "All right, so you do Mime, but which are you, an actor or a dancer?" But there are differences among these three, even though they all appear on a stage.

The actor is primarily verbal; the mime is not. Take away the actor's words, and he is a silent actor. We wait for him to commence talking again. Whatever his other virtues, and he may have many, the actor is judged by how well he manipulates his words, how well he creates a space in them for his acting. The actor approaches his text in the way a mime approaches his body. The actor makes plastic his words, flexing them, giving them tension, shaping them to give feeling and direction. As we have seen, this is what the mime learns to do with his body. Both produce the illusion of reality, but one has his hands and legs and torso to use, the other his voice and all of its sonorities.

To understand the weight of language for the actor, consider the production of a play in a foreign language. Although you may not grasp what is being said, the total effect of aural rhythms, intonations, pauses, and the rest will make sense. Now tune out the sound, as though this were television you were watching, and the production will lack sense. It does not simply lack comprehensible words; it lacks the sinuousness of language itself. The mime creates the sensuous forms of reality by first excluding sound. Words are to him objects, almost figurines which he could admit to his stage as he might an interesting stranger—with curiosity but caution. The prob-

156

lem for the mime is that the addition of words can sometimes break his illusion; the problem for the actor is that the absence of words can sometimes jeopardize his.

Dance would seem to be Mime's twin; after all, they both use the non-verbal body. But, despite appearances, Mime and dance are probably more clearly separated than Mime and acting. "Dance is evasion; Mime invasion," said Etienne Decroux. Dance can avoid the consciousness of knowing, for one can watch a dance without giving it meaning, or understanding its meaning. It is a celebration, in which "to celebrate" is the operating verb, bypassing our need to know, reinforcing our desire to participate and be. For this reason, dance, like music, is perhaps a purer form of the theatrical art. The shape is total; the relationship immediate; and therefore no mediation is required between the dancer and his audience.

Mime, on the other hand, must be comprehended. There must be consciousness. The mime fails when he is incomprehensible. Perhaps the dancer fails when he can too easily be comprehended, when his dance is too full of significance and articulate meaning. The dancer becomes heavy, too "verbose." In his turn, the mime who leans toward dance lightens his ability to make meaning and becomes equally heavy. His audience can only lose track of what he is saying.

The dancer, the actor, and the mime share the stage, but each takes a different part of it. Their angles of vision form a common triangle, but at the same time it keeps them separate. Each should know more about the particular visions of the other, but it is not enough merely to give the actor a little dance, the dancer a little acting, and for both of them a little Mime. One does not learn a new language by taking a short vacation in a foreign land.

The Event

An event is what happens; it may be an action or it may be a reaction. The mime walks, sits, looks, breathes, jumps, laughs, cries, or grabs; all of these are events. An event is the smallest particle of comprehensible movement. It must be easily recognizable. A shrug of the shoulders will mean something to the audience: it is an event. A lifted arm is not so easily definable—it may be a greeting, or a hand raised to ask a question, or an arm lifted to reach a light cord. Therefore it is not yet an event, only a movement. Starting with the event, the mime constructs his pantomime.

There are two ways to handle events. We may handle them in *chronology,* tacking one event onto another. Or we may do several events in *simultaneity.* The virtue in doing events in chronology is that it presents a clear and distinguishable order and logic. The audience is not confused, and the mime is not confused!

For example, let us say the

mime is writing, reading, and drinking. He may do each in turn, securely establishing each action: first a bit of writing, then some reading, and then a sip of wine. Each event, of course, consists of a number of sub-events— grabbing and releasing the pen, turning the pages of the book, and taking, lifting, and releasing the glass. There is much to be done in each event, but even the sub-events have their own sequence. For variety's sake, one can change the order of the chronology, sometimes drinking in between writing and reading,

sometimes looking up from the reading as though to go to another event, only to return to the page. However, events done in chronology ultimately seem monochromatic. It will be too much like playing the piano with one finger when one hears the possibilities of chords.

Life rarely takes place in order. We often do several things at once. We read with one hand, drink with the other. This is where the ability to do events simultaneously comes in. Chronology leads to clarity and order and creates the illusion of a well-

organized character, someone with a place for everything and everything in its place—someone a bit compulsive, perhaps. While simultaneity is necessary in the normal course of things, it opens the door to the hurried and frenzied and produces a somewhat more zany character.

Let's have a look at the new script: the mime writes, turns the pages as he drinks, puts down the glass as he writes, and so forth . . . until, eventually, everything is mixed up: the mime writes as he drinks, writes with his glass, drinks with his pen.

Simultaneity is harder to master than chronology. Confusion on stage—that is, planned confusion—is a question of careful organization and delicate handling. The mime has no excuse when it does not work; he has simply confused his audience. And confusing one's audience is different from showing confusion. Yet, difficult as simultaneity is to begin with, it is a necessary skill if one wishes to orchestrate feelings and meanings.

159

The Situation

A situation is an event that exists in a specific time and space. Usually, several events make a situation, as in our earlier example of writing, reading, and drinking. But one event can be a situation. A walk by itself is an event; placed in a concrete physical and temporal context, it becomes a situation. Situations focus events. I am in a situation when I walk *into* a place or *through* one or when my walk suggests the passage of time. The fabric of events has been cut and stitched into a dramatic pattern. The mime begins to make choices. He cannot do everything. He decides what he will do, what its order will be, and where it will take place. The audience feels comfortable with this deliberateness; it can see a plan and a direction. It can understand why one event follows the last, and it is willing to wait in order to discover what is going to happen next.

ACTIONS IN SPACE. Actions happen in space; but, in turn, they define that very space. As they occur, they set their own spatial limits. For this reason,

they not only happen in space but they are enclosed by a given space.

Let's look at an example: The mime eats at a table. He defines his space where the action takes place. To begin with, he is able to define only a limited space, the space created by his use of a table, a chair, and his eating utensils. We have no sense what the rest of the space looks like. Is he sitting inside a room or is he sitting on a pleasant outdoor terrace? Is he at home or in a restaurant? We just don't know. However, if the mime gets up and opens an imaginary refrigerator, taking out a can of beer, we know that the action takes place in his home. Or if he turns to an imaginary waiter to place an order, we know he is in a restaurant. So it goes.

The space takes on shape as the action unfolds. Thinking in terms of organizing space helps the mime compose his pantomime; the mime finds that he has developed something solid to lean on. His actions become more clearly defined because they are more clearly framed;

hence they can be more easily understood.

But action within a clearly framed space is not enough. The action must seem *credible* to the audience in terms of the space being used, and it must be *visible*. If the mime leaves his chair to move about and then returns to it, he cannot afford to miss the chair. His audience remembers where he has placed his imaginary chair and table; if he does not, it will seem as though he is sitting in empty space. Once more, we come up against the principle of fidelity. As we have seen in talking about touch and manipulation, if the mime does not honor fidelity, he loses his credibility.

No matter how credible a mime's use of space and how remarkable his manipulations are, if his actions cannot be seen, they amount to nothing. The mime gets up from his chair, goes to a refrigerator, and quite adroitly re-creates its insides, moving bottles, opening packages, and taking out an apple. Yet he does this with his back to the audience. All this dex-

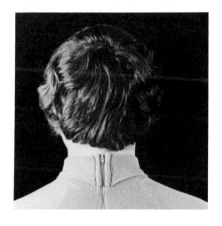

terity and imagination has been lost. Visibility is zero; understanding is zero.

To make himself visible, the mime learns to "center" himself. Like a potter who centers a piece of clay so that the centrifugal force of his wheel is evenly distributed, the mime puts himself in the center of the forces he is going to use. Often this means he must place himself at the center of his stage. However, don't take this as an iron-clad rule. Many exceptions are possible, even desirable. The important point is that centering is a necessity sufficiently strong to create its own need. If it means placing yourself in a corner of the stage, place yourself in a corner.

When a mime centers himself, he first must realize that everything is going to emanate from him; every action and reaction is going to radiate from him into the empty space. Accordingly, he has to know his spatial requirements so that he can organize his actions to keep himself at the psychological, if not real, center of the stage.

Consider how the novice and the more expert mime use space in an identical situation.

The scenario: The mime is in the street, comes into a building, opening a door, crosses through several rooms, reaches the last room, and discovers a treasure. The novice will start at the far side of the stage and move across the stage to reach the treasure at the other far side; he will end up almost in the wings. (Sometimes, in fact, I have seen a mime disappear into the wings, propelled somehow by the action.) By the time the treasure is discovered, a good third of his audience cannot see what is happening. There is a fair chance that the novice has also moved upstage during his traverse of the stage, cutting away still more of the visibility.

How did this happen? The novice did not center himself; instead he "cornered" himself.

Let's retrace his steps. He starts on the far side; there is nothing wrong with that. He goes into the first room; a few more steps and he will be in the second room. Everything is going fine. Once in the second room, he takes a few more steps to reach

the next room. He is still doing well, although space is becoming scarce. By the time he is through the third room, his working space is very tight. Before he knows it, he has crossed the whole width of the stage and has no place to go. He has been cornered by sheer inertia. He followed the space he had created, without daring to interfere, without realizing that his imaginary space could be bent at any time to suit his needs.

Our expert mime will also start at the far side of the stage. But, from the beginning, he will center himself: he will project his needs for space and act accordingly. As he reaches the second or third room, he will break the linear succession of the rooms; he will change directions as often as is necessary to bring himself finally to a well-centered treasure room.

This does not mean the mime has a well-rehearsed master plan in mind; one can occur to him as the action unravels. He is free to make decisions on the spot; he can locate doors and rooms as suit his purpose, as long as he

takes into account the total available empty space and aims at a final place that is both convenient and visible in which to discover the treasure. Probably he will locate the treasure center-stage, somewhere near the audience. The novice is often tempted to shy away from this spot, perhaps because he feels less protected there. But, after all, if one wishes to be a performer, one must be willing to be at the center of attraction.

ACTION IN TIME. The mime creates space; he spends time. Often he will pay a great deal of attention to how he creates space, but he forgets that he uses time. The space is his, and he has an ego involvement in it. Time, though, belongs to everyone. In particular, it belongs to the audience; the spectators are the ones who will feel that their time is being wasted. The mime can't afford to let this happen. It is always a sad moment when a mime is creative but boring. Of course, the mime must spend time, but he must spend it well.

The Silence

The mime moves in several dimensions. We know the three dimensions of space and the fourth dimension of time. There is another dimension the mime must consider: the dimension of silence. For, clearly, the mime, above all others, moves in silence. Even if he should finally add music, he still defines himself by having first mastered a voiceless and often soundless stage.

Silence, like time, is relative; it depends upon who is listening and where the listener is. The audience hears nothing because the mime has absorbed all of his sounds. His walk or his stomp across stage make no noise. A sneeze, a laugh, a clap, even his breathing are there but not to be heard, for if they were heard, his illusion would end. The mime creates a world, then, where the invisible approaches the inaudible.

The mime listens to the silence of his audience. A multitude of breaths more or less tensed, of hearts beating more or less in unison, of laughs, giggles, sighs, gasps do not interrupt the silence. Far from it. They give silence texture and meaning. They are like the crackling of a good fire, the mark of an appreciative and warm audience. The mime wants to nourish this fire, and to do so, he must listen attentively to the silences of his audience in order to sense its pulse and its rhythms. So, of all things, the mime must have a good ear. Jean-Louis Barrault once said that man "wrinkles" space; one could say that a mime wrinkles silence.

Actions are defined by the time it takes to do them. The difference between a quick drink and a slow one is not measured only in seconds; it is measured in meaning. It can be the difference between a shot and a sip, between having a friendly drink and taking some medicine. What is true for an individual motion is all the more true for actions in general. Speed and rhythm are the keys to live actions. They give actions their tempo, and that breaks the cautious monotony and presents the pulse of life.

Besides tempo, the mime has to consider how much time he wants to spend with a given action. How long should an action last before another one breaks in? This is a question of *timing*. There is probably no way to agree on what makes for the best timing in any given situation. It is easier to recognize bad timing —the smell of boredom is in the air. However, we can safely talk about adequate timing, sufficient to keep actions moving and to keep the interest of the audience alive.

163

Timing is hard to teach because it depends so much upon the mime's own sense of timing. The best guide is that he sharpen his sense of *necessity* and *sufficiency*. What is the least amount of time an action can last and still be meaningful? This is its necessary time. What is the most amount of time an action can last and still remain meaningful? This is its sufficient time.

By being aware there is a minimum time to put into an action as well as a maximum time, the mime has already gone some way toward understanding good timing. He can tighten his frame of reference. When hesitant about his own perception of time, he can either extend his action to meet necessity or shorten it to stay within sufficiency.

A delicate balance exists between the requirements of necessity and sufficiency. An action must have time to register and be understood. If a mime is writing and drinking, for instance, he will need to spend at least a few seconds on each action to make it clear. But clarity by itself is not enough; the action will seem too restricted, perhaps a bit jerky or timid. An act allowed to go on too long will saturate the audience with effects. The longer the audience waits, the more tense it becomes. At a certain moment, the mime must move on or lose everything. For most basic acts like writing or drinking, the mime will not need more than thirty seconds to establish sufficiency, and sometimes less will be enough.

The hallmark of the good mime is how he plays with this running edge. Know the limits of sufficiency and you can afford to go beyond them. A certain degree of expansiveness can fill out the moment. However, be careful about succeeding too well. A moment can be overwhelmed by too much stage presence. It is here that the mime turns virtuoso. To be sure, he receives applause, but he also jeopardizes the larger structure of his performance. Work instead for a pleasure—a sense of complicity —that can be shared but does not need to be expressed.

The Observation of a Barbarian on the Subject of Mime

A Barbarian, who finding the Subject required five Actors, and seeing but one Dancer, ask'd who should act, and personate the rest; and being inform'd that this one Dancer would perform the Whole; at the End of the Representation, told the Dancer, *I was mistaken in you, my Friend, who, tho' you have but one Body, have many Souls:* This was the Observation of the Barbarian.

> John Weaver, *A History of Mimes and Pantomimes* (London, 1728)

The Conflict

The mime should realize that all situations are not equally interesting; so much depends upon the cultural baggage we each carry about. On any night, the theater is crowded with a multitude of different assumptions and beliefs. Somewhere, though, there are common concerns, similar views of humor, or shared anxieties that include both the mime and his audience. It is the business of the mime to find them. To begin with, the mime takes into account both the nature of his history and the nature of his society. Then he can start to select among the wide range of possible situations those that speak to his heart and to his audience.

While all situations are not equally interesting, many can be made more interesting. Conflict is the tool that sharpens. It places opposites together to make a whole; it shows the con-

tradictions in seeming harmony. There are other tools to shape the drama and to be used in creating the final form of the pantomime, but conflict is the first, the most essential.

Let's consider the situation of a mime smoking. For a while this action can sustain the interest by itself. We have the magic of manipulating an invisible cigarette and the display of smoking, the gentle rhythms of inhaling and exhaling. A cigarette is more

than a smoke! But how long can a good thing last? Despite whatever hints of glamour or mystery cigarette smoking has, it is not a particularly strong action. Like most stereotypes, its immediacy cuts both ways: it is quickly recognizable, and it is quickly exhausted.

If this action is to work in any extended fashion, the mime must put it into a specific space and a specific time. Often when he finds the right space and the right

166

time, he will discover the ingredients for conflict. And this conflict may come about organically, out of the nature of the act; or it may arise when the act is confronted by a conflicting logic.

The act of smoking is simple; the longer one smokes, the shorter the cigarette becomes. So the act of smoking presents a problem—a small problem but still an interesting one. The mime wants to smoke this cigarette, as much of it as he can manage, but it gets smaller and smaller and more difficult to handle. The conflict is between the agility of his fingers and the perversity of the disappearing cigarette. The audience no longer asks the question: "Is anything going to happen?" Now there is a reason to wait: "How is it going to be solved?" The audience's natural curiosity has been challenged. Don't underestimate the inclination of the audience to take sides in any given fight, even if it is only between a mime and his invisible cigarette.

In addition to discovering a conflict within a situation, we may create one by placing the action in a context that makes it difficult to perform. A mime smokes. A policeman comes in. "No smoking on the premises," he says. The mime agrees and the policeman leaves. But the mime still wants to smoke, and he does. But now he is afraid of being caught; he is cautious, looking around for the policeman, hiding his activity, increasingly nervous. In short, he is in conflict with his surroundings, with his space.

In the first example, the mime created a situation by looking into the action, exploiting the conflict between time and desire —the longer he smoked, the shorter the cigarette, and the more he wanted to keep smoking. In the second example, the mime looked outside the situation to bring in a conflict, a conflict in this case between space and desire.

As you can see, conflict gives texture to the flat and the uneventful. How each mime is going to face up to any given conflict is another story. Like any fight, the battle rarely goes by the book. Each performer will have to draw from his personal experiences. He will use every trick of his trade and discover some he did not know he had. In particular, he will have to draw on his imagination, wit, sense of humor as well as his sense of the tragic, his naïveté, and his sophistication. As for a general formula to handle a conflict, I'm sorry, there is none. The most important thing to understand about conflict is that it can be a key to unknown doors that open on unexpected encounters.

8. The Uses of Imagination

Mime, more than any other art, requires creativity of its performer because the mime is so totally alone when he is on stage. He has no text to memorize and deliver, no music to lean on, only a loose plot or a vague idea. Often as not, he has nothing at all, especially when he first starts. He is not only the performer; he is also his own script writer and director. Unfortunately, the tools we have met so far do not secure creativity. Probably nothing does. But some activities, more than others, can help develop the creative sense.

What follows are two approaches to the problem of creating a larger form out of the pantomime elements we have already talked about. The first is improvisation; it opens up style, showing directions to move in and ideas to build upon. The second approach takes advantage of established aesthetic forms and styles. Ultimately, there is no true division between these two approaches. Improvisation springs out of what you already know of other people's work.

169

The tradition of forms is never static; the mime improvises as he uses a traditional form; sometimes he collapses one form into another, and sometimes he thinks of a way to give a new twist to an old and dry meaning. Behind all this hovers inspiration, the lucky or shrewd flash that gives life to whatever one is doing. Don't work at being inspired; work at the craft. Inspiration will come. It will!

Games and Entertainment

Children create and re-create reality for themselves. A stick becomes a magic wand or a gun; a place in a tree becomes a secret home; a game of hide-and-seek, a mystery of invisibility and great adventure. It is through games that children discover the world and make their place in it, imitating the adults in their lives and creating subtle variations for themselves.

Let us not over-romanticize the child, but let us not forget the early wonder of a world made new every day. Crude and prosaic things were transformed into marvelous objects and into strange and wonderful creatures, quite beyond anything modern technology could make.

The spirit behind the games of children is the desire to discover, the search for the unexpected, and the delight in returning to something familiar but now in a new form. As we get older, we seem to lose this ability to play freely with the unexpected and make it our own. What used to be active imagination blurs into fantasy and dimly recollected dreams. Our games are consciously set outside our normal life; we "go out" to play. We have a game of cards or watch

170

Improvisation

others play for us at football games or baseball games. There is still, of course, the game buried at the heart of everyday life, the game we play as we each live our particular version of Balzac's *Comédie Humaine*. But it is an unconscious game that follows the rules of social behavior.

What began as the marvelous in our childhood ends as simple entertainment. God's Spell, the gospel of good tidings told by friend to friend and told to oneself, has been transformed into gossip, the false chatter between strangers. Somewhere along the line, somehow, we have lost our delight. We created distances between ourselves and our imagination and are often too blasé. The French say "blasé" for "blunted." It is as though, instead of sharpening us, life has made us dull. Perhaps. In any case, the test of one's youth is the degree to which one does not become blunted to the games within oneself.

The mime must fight the same struggle. He attempts to reconcile the entertaining with this lost marvelous, and he does it for his own sake as well as for the sake of his audience.

The forms of improvisation are the forms of games. One plays according to rules, but one is never quite sure what will happen. The moment of surprise is often the moment of discovery. The three Mime games I present here are basic games to develop skill in improvising. You should feel free to improvise new games from these games or think of entirely new ones.

The virtue of the games is that each provides a frame for students to participate in. They are deliberately restrictive so that there is a clear limit to what can be done, since the major problem with creativity is that it tempts one to do everything at once. This is the Odyssey Complex, a common trap for the novice mime. He wants to show everything that comes to mind. It is a natural impulse that comes alive as the creative powers bubble to the surface. The novice is saying, "Look at all the things I can think of!" But it should be avoided at all cost; it dilutes the action and weakens the chain of events.

171

PICK UP AND FOLLOW. The participants (generally between six and twelve) sit in a semi-circle facing an empty space. The rules: The first player is to get up and start miming, establishing a situation, and then freeze. (The situations should be brief, well within a minute; there is no need to attempt to develop the situation fully.) The second player then steps in, as shortly as possible after the first player's freeze, and "picks up" the situation. He continues it, but develops it according to his own fancy so as to establish, as briefly as the first player, a new situation; then he freezes. Each player, in turn, carries on in the same fashion. One need not follow any particular order of participation. Whoever wishes to perform first can; whoever wishes to follow should. The freeze can be handled in two ways. Each player can remain in his position, keeping his freeze until all the participants are frozen into one tableau. Or each player can delicately go back to his seat, fading away as the next player picks up the situation.

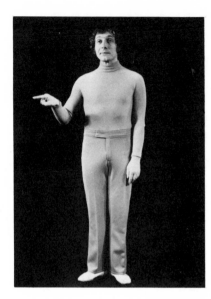

172

The game scatters the responsibility; players do not have the burden of performing a complete pantomime, so they feel freer to perform and experiment with their moment. The first player has the most difficult job; he must initiate something. The players after him have something to focus their imagination on. Having something to follow may at first seem to be a tedious obligation, but it can be a great help; it provides a real incentive to perform.

PICK UP AND TWIST. This game is a variation of Pick Up and Follow. The rules are slightly changed; one more limit is added: When a player picks up a situation, he is not permitted to develop it; he must distort it, twisting the already established meaning. For example, the first player walks, stops, checks a name on a door, then rings a bell, freezing his finger as he reaches the invisible bell. The second player could have followed the first player, becoming the host who came to the door to answer the bell and greet his guest. Instead he backs into the finger frozen in mid-air, thinks it is a gun in his back, and raises his hands as if he were being held up. Each of the other players follows in this manner.

WHAT-WHEN-WHERE or "The W's." One player volunteers. He asks the group to give him a what, a when, or a where. His audience gives him an object or a location or a moment in time. He mimes what he is given as quickly as possible.

From games such as these, the amateur should realize that improvisation is an open-ended process; it is a controlled search where one is free to feel his way. One must maintain a state of open readiness if this search is to be rewarding. Readiness is all! But do not be ready with something in mind to do, rather be ready to do something, anything. It is hard to be without preconceptions; but if these exercises teach anything, they will teach you how to avoid the pitfalls of the preconceived. A preset idea often obstructs more than it helps. It gets in the way, making it impossible to see what is really happening.

There is a trick to improvising that entails balancing oneself between being open to future possibilities and focusing on the present action. The mime learns to *lean* in his present action until he feels well supported by it. This gives him the time to flesh it out, to give it the rich detail that makes it seem real. He finds that the richness of the present stimulates his imagination; the reality of the act itself will suggest a new act, a new direction.

This is the way to create a chain of improvised events: Let the solid detail of the immediate event lead your imagination. The focus on specifics will not restrict you. It will do quite the reverse. You will find that you have a relaxed stability, a center from which you can think and move.

Here is an example of the process: I am open. An idea comes or a theme is offered: I start to eat an apple. I focus my attention and my skill on this action, putting myself entirely in the present moment of eating an apple. Yet, I am still open. As

173

my present grows secure, is clear, well established, and convincing even to me, I become ready for something else to happen. And it happens. The apple may stick in my throat or it may be rotten or I may throw the remaining piece away . . . or whatever. It is all a question of one step at a time, but each step must be a well-formed step. It will give you the balance to achieve the next one.

THE GROUP. After the mime has learned to improvise by himself, he will want to learn to improvise with others. The lessons of individual improvisation remain perfectly valid, but working with someone else in the same space and time will add some specific problems. In the first place, the mime now has more than one audience to communicate with; he must understand what his partner wants and make himself clear to his partner as well as continue to make himself clear to the audience beyond the lights. In the second place, he has to adapt his ideas to the new situation. Now that he is not alone, he is not in total author-

ity. He cannot dictate what he wants or be absolutely sure what he will be given. He will give and he will get; and he must be able to handle what he gets as well as control what he gives.

Let us consider a simple scene improvised by two. The first mime establishes that he is drinking at a bar. In walks the second mime, who takes on the role of a barman. So far, so good. This scene may now develop along several very different lines. This is where it gets interesting.

The classic line of action follows the customer getting drunk. In turn, the barman wants to kick him out; the customer resists; and a fight breaks out. This scene is classic because there is an easy chain of cause and effect; each action and reaction picks up from the previous action. The direction of the action is quickly apparent to both mimes. A more difficult line of action is this: The customer drinks silently; as he drinks, he becomes progressively inert and

174

impassive. The barman tries to cheer him up and ends by joining him in a few drinks. The barman gets drunk.

Whatever line an improvisation follows, each step of the action brings new propositions from each player. Each player in turn must understand the proposition of his partner, then accept or reject it, opening up space for his partner to act in. For such scenes to stay readable, clear, and interesting, the mimes naturally need their basic solo skills.

But, in addition, they will need a good sense of how to work together. Without this, they will miss each other's actions: the barman will, for example, pour a drink into a glass that has already been removed. Or they will employ a confusing and exaggerated mixture of hand and head motions in order to signal their intentions to each other. The effect will not be Mime but that of a dumbshow in which buffoons make speechless nods and tugs to communicate.

To develop this ability to play together, the game Pick Up and Follow is quite helpful. In order to make it an improvisation for more than one, each player continues his action and role when the next player comes in, instead of freezing in place. Pick Up and Follow should first be tried as a duet; only after the relationships have had a chance to be explored should other players be added. Even then, each new player enters only after there is a solid structure for him to enter. This is important because improvisation for several is a delicate task requiring great tact. The

most frequent result of working together is confusion; going slow will help maintain control.

Notwithstanding his skill as a soloist, the mime will need to reorder his priorities. First, he will have to give priority to his mate, for the pantomime is no longer a matter of give and make, as it is in a solo performance, nor even a matter of give and take, but more a matter of give and give. He must keep giving his unrestricted attention to what his partner is up to. He must allow his partner to have priority in the actions he is developing.

If you give priority to the other fellow, he gives priority to you. When all follow this rule, an undercurrent of care and attention (not to say mutual respect) is created that makes possible and credible the most improbable situations. Shared priorities take away the edge of aggressiveness that is the mark of a novice trying to affirm himself and allow real interaction to take place. As more players improvise together, giving priority becomes even more important because the initiative for an action can come

from any one of a number of directions, thickening the possibility of confusion.

Once having established the ability to work with other mimes, the mime can begin to plan a *mimodrama,* a drama in Mime. Presenting dramatic relationships between various Mime characters is an option the mime will want to use from time to time, for there will be things he wants to say that can best be said in conjunction with other mimes. He should not forget, though, that much can be said and done in a solo performance. There is the temptation to hide in a crowd, just as there is the temptation to take over the whole stage for oneself. The mime has to judge his intentions carefully in order to decide whether mimodrama or solo is most appropriate.

The problem the beginning mime confronts, whether he works alone or with other mimes, is that he is afraid he will be left with nothing to do, so he plans too far ahead and rushes what he is doing. His improvisations become pallid and shabby; his rhythms become jerky and unnatural.

For the mime, improvisation is the threshold of artistic creation. It teaches the necessity to *select* and it develops the ability to *emphasize.* Out of improvisation, the mime learns how to be playful. The more relaxed he is, the more space and time he can freely give himself. He will not need to grab for the obvious or the cliché, taking what he can because he is afraid he will have nothing to hang on to. There is always something there if he moves on solid ground.

The group can help focus direction, intensify emotions, and develop interactions. Two pictures from *Men and Dreams;* the third from *Renard.*

Law of Economy

A lot of theory becomes concrete when one puts theory into practice. I have talked about visibility and credibility, about necessity and sufficiency, about selection and emphasis. In all of this, I have stressed the importance of the principle of clarity—the importance of making actions easily understood. After a few tries at improvising or watching others improvise, I think you will see more clearly why these principles are important. We can collect all of these principles under one basic law: the law of economy.

Perhaps it seems amusing to talk about economy in art. When society is being economical, it has very little use for art. Art is the grand superfluity. Who cares about it when one is hungry, except the hungry artist? In any case, those who care about art often talk about the virtues of "pure art," or "simplicity," or "style." Each term, in its own way, speaks to the state of economy: the management of the parts so that the whole will be discernible and harmonious. That is what art is all about.

180

Freedom and Boredom

The mime controls the stage, and while he is on it, he can do what he wants. But there is always the audience—at least, one hopes there is—and the audience has its rights. The artist wants to be free to do what he wants; the audience, in its turn, doesn't want to be bored. A good mime will be sensitive to the yawns and fatigue of his audience even as he tries to stretch his own freedom to its limits.

It is foolish to idealize one's audience, just as it is foolish to idealize one's own rights as an artist. The point in theater is that a collaboration is going on, in this case between the mime and his audience. An evening of good theater is entertaining, but at its best it is something more than that. In order to get beyond the sheer fun of an entertaining evening, the mime must perform at his highest level without being lured by a false sense of freedom. At the same time, he should not become a buffoon simply to satisfy his audience.

Too much freedom on the mime's part separates him from his audience. Too much buffoonery separates the audience from itself.

The audience, on its part, must be willing to let its expectations change and grow. It will find itself passing from the effortless appreciation of a good joke—basically passive even if expressed by a loud belly laugh—to a more active appreciation where humor may be more silent but more gentle and rich. Both the mime and his audience will have to concentrate. Still, this new density will bring them together, leaving them both with the feeling that an experience has been shared and that something new has been achieved.

The law of economy is simple: Get the most for the least, but do not become a miser! William Blake, the English poet, put the issue another way: "Enough or too much." You have a choice: present enough *or* present too much. The problem with presenting too little is obvious; there will not be enough to see. But the problem with giving too much is a little less obvious. Too much goes beyond the bounds of sufficiency, making the stage too busy for the audience's eyes. Like most laws, it is an easy one to state but a hard one to carry out. That is why improvisation is so useful; it will show you how too much of an action destroys meaning rather than adding to it.

There are two kinds of uneconomy. The first repeats an act or extends it. A single nod of the head is a thoughtful yes. By using a series of nods, a mime will alter this meaning and change the mood of the action. A series reflects enthusiasm, nervousness, or eagerness to agree, all meanings very different from that of a single thoughtful nod. The second kind of uneconomy uses two

actions when one is sufficient. If one nod will do, a nod plus hand-clapping will not do, for a new meaning will have been created.

The right action done for the right amount of time is truer and more powerful than one over-done, or two added together. More is not better! Economy is not a matter of conserving energy. It is a matter of getting the intended results and projecting the precise personality and mood that one has in mind. To be economical, one must know what it is one wants to say; then it is a question of hitting the target with one arrow. That is what makes a mime performance impressive. Overkill is not an art.

Actions do not have any intrinsic value; economy is what gives value. An unnecessary gesture or too many gesticulations can smother an act, blur the clarity, or weaken the meaning. Gesticulation can hamper an overzealous actor; but it kills a mime, for his audience will become lost in the complexity of his motions, seeing only details and not seeing actions. So the mime has to take a hard look at

his activity. He becomes selective. He will not hesitate to throw away the unneeded in order to keep the essential.

An act boiled down to its essentials can be quite forceful. For example, in a pantomime called "The Village," an old schoolmaster points to a student, calling him to the blackboard. The old man moves nothing except his crooked index finger. He is an imposing statue, all the more imposing because he is unbending. All the meaning is condensed into that one finger; it is a hook pulling the student forward. The tension thus created is palpable; the moment is dense. Any other motion would not only be unnecessary but would blur and diffuse this tension. The little motion of the finger is both economical and powerful. All attention is focused on it: the attention of the child, of the class, and of the audience.

It is by drawing together such energy that economy produces its special power. The mime discovers that "little" is not synonymous with "weak" nor "big" synonymous with "strong." Rather,

181

strength is energy well channeled, concentrated and focused in a specific direction. And weakness is scattered energy or, of course, no energy at all. To some degree, what I am talking about could be called the ecology of Mime. This is the principle that says that the size and energy of a movement or an action should not be wasted.

What is true for the individual action is equally true for the larger situation. There must be economy within the total situation so that actions do not get in the way of each other. This economy entails a global vision of the action so that one can determine the relative value of each individual action. Some very nice details may have to be cut or diminished in order to achieve the correct proportions.

A good example of the global point of view at work can be found in the pantomime "The Bottle." A drunk is caught in a growing bottle. He fights desperately to stop it from "swallowing" him. But, ultimately, it is too late—he is completely inside the bottle. He realizes the situation with a pathetic pause and starts to hammer on his prison.

In this situation, all the actions and psychological nuances have to be subordinated to the global ideas of desperate struggle and pathetic imprisonment. The face is not allowed to grimace; it has but one basic expression, that of anxiety. The body does not move wildly; a very few movements are concentrated into one effort, that of the struggle. Over all, there is no indulgence. The struggle leads to the pause; the pause leads to the hammering. Each stage of action could have been allowed to

evolve on its own, but the whole sequence would have been weakened. The economy of the structure enables the mime to reach a certain harmony in which all of the parts combine to make a graceful and sensitive whole.

One final aspect of the law of economy is the ability not to be self-deceived. It is too easy to believe that everything one has thought of is worth saying. A well-developed sense of economy gives one a constructive modesty. A mime's power to suggest is relative and depends on his ability to recognize what works and what does not work. The fatal trap closes on the mime when he is hypnotized by his own magic. After all, he is trying to be suggestive to his audience and not to himself. He must be ready to take out what he likes but does not find useful.

The Tradition of Forms

Being in control does not bring about ideas. Where does the mime turn to find sources of inspiration? Of course, he should start with himself and his own particular perception of life. Often he will stumble on a truth. Improvisation will help him find connections between one odd perception and what seemed to be another totally unrelated one. Aristotle described this as the ability to make metaphor—the ability to yoke dissimilars together. This is the skill of the mime, as it is the skill of all artists.

Tradition itself is a source of inspiration. Every time we see a performance, read a book, or look at a movie, we think of how we might have done it differently or we think of ways to take one part of the form and insert it in another.

Strictly speaking, Mime has no tradition of its own forms. It is the great borrower. It can incorporate a great deal and move with ease between different moods and genres. Perhaps it is a defect of Mime, perhaps it is its virtue, but Mime is not rigor-

Cinema and Television

From still photographs through flip-books to movies and television, the direction of the visual has been toward movement. Until the talkies appeared and took over, cinema and Mime were very much in the same family: each making meaning by using movement. Granted, movies did use sets and props; yet the important center of silent films was the subject, and many of the actors who portrayed these subjects were masters of Mime technique, especially the technique of the Mime of the Subject. And what subjects! Charlie Chaplin, Buster Keaton, Harold Lloyd each in his own way used his body to achieve emotional tones that made words unnecessary, even if they had been possible in their medium.

Television has, of course, produced some great mimes, or comedians who use Mime techniques. The range is wide, from Sid Caesar's brilliant and extensive use of Mime in his *Show of Shows,* to Red Skelton, who combined Mime and vaudeville, to Danny Kaye, Dick Van Dyke, Jonathan Winters, Lucille Ball, and Carol Burnett. Even the masters of the talk-show format—Jack Parr, Johnny Carson, Dick Cavett, and William Buckley—use Mime gestures, double takes, and physical reactions to make transitions, to frame episodes, to comment, and to redirect conversation.

The influence has been two-way. Cinema and television have learned much from the art of Mime; and mimes have learned much by seeing what the camera can do to events and timing. Perhaps the greatest influence upon contemporary Mime has been that of Chaplin. It is difficult to find a mime in the last half-century who is not in debt to him in some way, for his style, or his gags, or the kinds of conflict he developed. His acting itself sets an example and a standard for other mimes to follow. His use of Disposition Zero is subtle. His body is always ready to move in any direction, and this physical flexibility, in turn, suggests a psychological flexibility.

His character, "the noble tramp," ambles into each new event, taking whatever position is required without prejudice and, seemingly, without preparation. Using the restrictions of silent acting, Chaplin often moved directly into Mime itself. In *The Pilgrim,* he mimes the story of David and Goliath before a congregation of churchgoers. In *The Gold Rush,* the actor Chaplin transforms himself into a chicken as his hungry, snowbound cabin mate begins to imagine that Charlie is eatable. In *Modern Times,* he plays a singing waiter who has lost his lyrics and is forced to sing and mime in French gibberish. It is, I think, impossible to like Mime and not to like Chaplin!

Movies no longer are wedded to silence, and television never was. Still, movies and television have much in common with Mime. They are all committed to visual details. The investigating eye of the camera frames events in ways quite similar to those of the mime: the attention of the audience is focused at certain points and not at others. The freeze, the slow motion, the quick cut from one scene to another are techniques that all three employ. Take, for example, a scene in which a character is responding to events off camera. We see only him; we imagine what he is reacting to. If the frame of the camera were to collapse—or if the camera were to zoom back—we would probably see that the actor is acting alone, playing to an empty space. And we would know that he too has been miming.

ous in its use of forms. It does not need to follow the form of tragedy or comedy, nor need it delimit clear beginnings, middles, and ends. Quite often, in fact, a pantomime starts in the middle of things and ends in the middle of things, somewhat like a dream. For all of these reasons, Mime is a highly flexible means of expression.

To give the beginning student of Mime a sense of the forms he can work with, I shall give a thumbnail sketch of some of the forms most often used. But he should not feel restricted by my outline. As his ability grows, he will want to piece together several forms into one pantomime. He will find a continuity for what he does as long as he has a clearly articulated vision.

Anecdotal or *narrative* mime is the most common pantomime; it stands closest to the structure of drama or cinema. The anecdotal pantomime presents a series of vignettes, while the narrative has a more elaborated plot. However, both convey a story by representing a palpable reality on which the mime often

185

Symbolic Mime: The Crowd. *Opus Blue . . . Is Pink.*

Symbolic Mime: Point of View. *Opus Blue . . . Is Pink.*

186

comments. Examples of these two kinds of pantomime are legion: "The Life Guard," "The Boxer," "Main Street," "The Painter," "The Public Park," "The Bus Ride." As you can see by these titles, sometimes the mime plays one character; at other times he plays a string of characters in order to create an environment.

In a *symbolic* or *metaphoric* pantomime, the mime is more interested in a subject or a problem than a story. Examples of this kind of pantomime are Marcel Marceau's life cycle, in which we see a man move from birth through youth, maturity, old age, and finally death, or "The Crowd," a group pantomime performed by my company, in which we see individuals lose and give up their identity in an octopus-like mass.

The *satirical* is rarely absent from a pantomime. Often it is the supporting element in a pantomime; frequently, though, it is the dominant mood. It is hard to say why satire is so well suited to Mime. Perhaps it is because the human is so completely iso-

lated and exposed in the empty space of Mime, and therefore foibles are isolated too. It is this that makes Mime only a gesture away from caricature and parody. If done well, Mime can present the image of the forgotten commonplace so that we are stunned by reperceiving its essentials. The mime stirring a cup of coffee makes us see it anew because we see the act and not the cup. When the everyday loses its normal backdrop, we take a new look at it. However, this must be done quite subtly. What is exposed is stark. If done heavily, it falls short of rich caricature and creates burlesque.

Sometimes the mime creates non-human forms on stage. This is called *figurative* pantomime or *animation*. There is a long history of the mime animating objects or plants or personifying animals. Decroux, the great French mime, made important inroads in this field. His pantomimes covered such topics as "The Covering," in which a sheet takes on life, or "The Factory," in which several mimes played the parts of an operating ma-

chine, or "The Statue." Lotte Goslar, a fascinating mime, produced "The Flower" in a captivating figurative pantomime. Dressed as a flower, she replayed a vegetal life cycle, sprouting, growing, facing various kinds of weather, and ultimately dying. Chaplin reversed the equation. In *The Gold Rush,* he animated two bread rolls so that they were transformed into a pair of dancing legs—quite sensitive and witty legs at that. Unlike most mimes, he became the puppeteer instead of the puppet.

There are two ways to handle the problem of becoming an object. One can be the object—that is, be a tree or a flower. Or one can take over the role of the object. For example, I remember a performance in which we asked for suggestions from the audience for improvisation. "Let's have a stomach," someone yelled. Instead of *being* a stomach, a member of the company quite cleverly envisioned himself inside the stomach and acting as the stomach's organ of intelligence. He caught food as it came down the throat, missing it occa-

Satirical Mime: The Cabinet Minister. *Men and Dreams.*

188

sionally or being hit in the eye by it. He packed it down, and shoveled it into the intestines. This was a more effective way of personifying the stomach than if he had taken the shape of the stomach. But it will depend upon the object being worked with. Some objects are better done from the outside.

There is something called *abstract* pantomime. I am not persuaded it is a true form of Mime; it belongs more to dance. (See the discussion of the *Triangle*, page 156.) An abstract pantomime is too ambiguous. Its individual parts and actions have no clearly defined meanings, although the entire pattern makes a general sense. Too much is left to interpretation. This contradicts the very nature of Mime. Mime is an explicit art, or at least it should be. It fails when the performer and his audience cannot agree on what is being done.

Another form of pantomime, the *surrealistic,* may seem to be only a version of abstract pantomime, but it is quite different.

The surreal presents clear and distinct images and actions, to begin with, and shuffles their order and rearranges their logic so that an entirely unexpected sequence appears—one that is not always immediately comprehensible. In contrast to the abstract, the parts of the surreal are familiar and quite explicit. It is the whole that we find unfamiliar.

This is a fascinating pantomime to work with because it explores the meaning of absurd connections, making them seem plausible and true. The game Pick Up and Twist will open the way into the surreal. After each player twists the meaning of the action, he continues with the logic of his action, instead of freezing for the next player.

Let us remember the example from the original game of Pick Up and Twist. A man rings the doorbell; a second man feels the finger in his back and thinks he is being held up. Two different points of view are in operation: the man ringing the doorbell continues to ring, not aware he

is ringing the shoulderblade of another man; the other man continues to assume he is being held up. Perhaps there is no clear sense in these two actions taken together, but there is a certain lucid madness in them that is appealing, if not immediately comprehensible.

In all of these examples of the uses of form and imagination, it is easy to lose sight of the whole as one struggles to say something on stage. The meticulous novice mime will take as his gospel: Be clear and simple. An admirable commandment. Yet if taken to the extreme, his simplicity can rapidly disintegrate into a naïveté in which details are permitted to flourish and ideas disappear. Such timidity should be avoided. To be sure, be simple, but do not be simpleminded.

On the other hand, the passionate, visionary novice mime is tempted to go in the other direction. He cultivates the great idea and underestimates the virtues of the little detail. It is difficult to find greatness in the little things

Figurative Mime: Goat and Cat. *Renard.*

190

of the everyday, but it is easy to lose it in the ready-made great idea.

To the visionary, details seem too mundane, too commonplace, so he mimes a slogan rather than making clear the nuances of his vision. Mimed jargon is no better than screamed polemics, although the former may be a bit more restful. Do not hide from great and important concerns, but be careful to make the idea new and the meaning rich.

Unhappily, great ideas all too often look better on monuments than on the stage, so the mime must approach them with caution. One way to know whether you have fallen into a trap is to look at your pantomime without its title. Titles are helpful, but they should not be allowed to become crucial. If your pantomime could not survive without a title like "Civilization," "Evolution," or "Revolution," you need to reconsider it. If the audience understands only the title and not the pantomime itself, you are in trouble. A pantomime should not work equally well under the title "Revolution" and "Mime of the Seven Veils," and some pantomimes do.

Finally, there is a perverse complicity between the mime and his audience which mimes must be careful of. The audience is all too ready to settle for bewilderment when confronted by a great idea. Profundity seems to make us willing to be bored, as long as we can feel intelligent. Although the mime and his audience applaud each other at the end of the piece, they have lost each other during the performance.

What the mime puts into his performance will depend a great deal upon where he looks for his material. There are mimes who live very creatively in the real world. Their pantomime is essentially *realistic,* for they have a sane logic which we quickly recognize. Even their renderings of the most extraordinary fairy tales follow the order and rules of everyday reality. There are other mimes who live deeply in their fantasies. They do not see a world of order and sense; they see a world of dreams and strangely connected shapes. Their pantomime is *fantastic.*

Generally speaking, the mime who feels comfortable with the realistic will use narrative, anecdotal, or satiric forms to structure his pantomimes, while the mime of the fantastic will use symbolic, figurative, or surrealistic forms. But there is no reason why these two temperaments should be kept separated. A figurative pantomime can have elements of the anecdotal, and a piece of satire can incorporate the symbolic.

For my part, I believe that the two temperaments—or perhaps they are visions—need each other. The realistic mime gains by being a little fantastic, as does the fantastic mime by being realistic. The beginning mime will want to find the value of each approach in its own right. But he should not stop there. He should learn to mix them together. He will enrich his own vision, and he will make the performance more interesting to watch.

Figurative Mime: The Sun. *The Legend of the Stonecutter.*

193

9. The Mime: His Limits and His Liberties

The skills of the mime are solo skills. He is a man alone. Even if he performs with other mimes, uses scenery, adds music to his productions, he stands by himself.

Why is that? The essential silence of the stage, the concentration of meaning in each movement, and the refined simplification of gestures—in short, all the machinery of re-creating a reality—expose the mime. The history of modern Mime is an attempt to come to grips with this fundamental nakedness of the mime on stage.

Jean Dorcy observes that the crucial contribution of the two great fathers of modern Mime, Etienne Decroux and Jean-Louis Barrault, is that they "reject[ed] all external help; acting naked on a naked stage, dispensing with a narrator and with musical support or accompaniment, and thus proving that the gesture can be self-sufficient."*

* *The Mime.* New York: Robert Speller & Sons, 1961.

195

This emphasis upon self-sufficiency is the watershed that distinguishes modern Mime from all earlier Mime. It announces the re-birth of Mime, making it a new art with a new language. Having gone this far, it will be hard for Mime to turn back. Although music and narration can be re-added to Mime, the self-sufficiency of the body is now the first given. The mime has responsibilities because he has developed expectations.

Nothing will now redeem his work except his own performance—not the words, not the lyrics, not the plot. Nothing. Each mime must be a soloist, ready to be the first mime of his company, be it a company of one or a company of half a dozen. His stage has no empty spaces and no empty moments when he can pause to catch his breath or gather his wits. Each illusion must be total, must be perfect, or it is no illusion at all. His gestures must be self-sufficient, no matter what else he now brings on stage with him. For this reason—because Mime is inherently a solo art, even when performed

big pillow. Cushion? *Looks* like cushion . . ." This well-meaning participation often upsets the true lover of silent theatre, and I have noticed a tendency on such occasions for those sitting next to me to express uneasiness in various forms, ranging from significant throat-clearings to a lion's-paw swipe on the back of the head, which I once received from a member of a Manhasset housewives' theatre party. On this occasion, a dowager resembling Ichabod Crane snapped her lorgnette quirtlike across my knuckles, with the admonition "Cool it, stud." . . .

Finally, the mime began blowing glass. Either blowing glass or tattooing the student body of Northwestern University, but it could have been the men's choir—or a diathermy machine—or any large, extinct quadruped, often amphibious and usually herbivorous, the fossilized remains of which have been found as far north as the Arctic. By now, the audience was doubled up with laughter over the hijinks on the stage. . . . But for me it was hopeless; the more I tried, the less I understood. A defeated weariness stole over me, and I slipped off my loafers and called it a day. The next thing I knew, a couple of charwomen at work in the balcony were batting around the pros and cons of bursitis. . . .

by a company—I have dwelt upon the means of acquiring these skills throughout this book.

This solitude of the mime provides him with a degree of liberty. If he is alone, if he refuses to share the stage with others, he is free, free to make the stage his own. Or so it seems. But is the mime really free? His own body is his first limit. He will discover that there are things he cannot express when he is alone. He cannot stage the complex and rich conflict between two equal characters, especially if that conflict demands simultaneous reactions from both characters.

To be sure, many solo mimes are noted for their ability to create characters in sequence, filling the stage with a number of individual characters. But here the audience is presented only with a series of personalities,

197

each one physically independent from the others, linked together usually by a common setting, like a public park or a main street. When well done, this is a virtuoso piece that should not be underestimated in its ability to charm and delight. Still, the audience has only an isolated view of each character; there is neither time nor need to relate him completely to those who come before and after.

Despite the exceptions we can think of, the solo mime's seesaw between characters can become labored and confusing. If the mime wishes to have equally weighted characters confronting each other directly within the same space, he must know when to give up his solitude and invite another mime on stage.

For instance, once when I was staging a Mime performance of Stravinsky's *L'Histoire du Soldat*, I came to the famous card-playing sequence between the devil and the soldier. It was important to have the two characters play to each other: the soldier with his personality, his fears, and his growing confi-

dence, and the devil with his charm, trickery, and bravado, all ultimately turned against him. A solo performance at this point would have been an impressive *tour de force*, but the drama would have suffered.

What is clear is that the mime must be careful not to succumb to the exhilaration of performing by himself on stage. And there *is* an exhilaration! It comes when the power of his illusions is absolute, an absoluteness that is possible only when he shares the stage with no one and nothing. There is a certain magic in this. The mime is the magician whom we can't take our eyes off, since so much hangs on his ability to make his illusion work.

There is also a certain degree of ease for the mime in being alone, for he need not concern himself with any tempo other than his own. The structure, the space, and time are his. Nothing has to be divided. Nevertheless, however tempting it is to do a solo performance, it is a temptation that should be controlled. Sometimes it is highly appropriate; sometimes, though, it

limits and weakens his art, as well as diminishing his vision. By himself, the mime is limited to himself. He can say more and often learn more by adding others.

WHEN THE MIME WORKS with music, scenery, costumes, and other mimes, the mime widens the scope of his performance. Perhaps he does lose some of his power as he loses his personal control over his audience, but he is compensated for this by an increased richness and texture not always obtainable in a solo.

His possibilities are multiplied, and new sources of inspiration can be tapped. By adding music, he heightens his oral sense, a sense as necessary for dealing with silence as it is for sound. By adding scenery, he will find that he can highlight the effects of his body differently, not clouding its power but enhancing it. For instance, in "Eve and the Serpent," if one does not use the tree prop, the isolation between the arm and the rest of the body will not be satisfactorily complete. And without a total

The Card Game. *L'Histoire du Soldat.*

Costumes can vary greatly in texture, bulk, and complexity. In the same piece
(*Au Clair de la Lune*), the astronauts wear material that has been bolted together;
the pierrots wear the loosely flowing gowns of the nineteenth century clown.

isolation, one will not see two characters—the snake and Eve —interacting with each other.

I do not suggest that all Mime be group Mime or multi-media Mime. Far from it. A high level of tact will always be necessary. The mime should not drop the solo performance as an impulsive reaction to the established expectations of his audience. Neither should he pick up all the paraphernalia of mixed media simply because it is fashionable. He should be open. He must feel the logic of what is to be said and be free to recognize the limits of one mode in order to gain the liberties of another.

There will be those who will feel that Mime which includes more than the mime's own body is impure. By this, I suppose they mean that the imaginary is no longer total. But is the imaginary ever really total when the performer faces his audience? The mime's very presence spoils the purity of the imagination. Pure Mime would have to be an empty stage facing an imaginative audience. Even then the stage and its frame would be

real. Perhaps only the reverse would make Mime pure: a real audience with its eyes closed at an imagined theater.

As a quick history of antique Mime shows, Mime is not pure. The question for modern Mime is only in its priorities; it begins by demonstrating the importance of controlling the body and its meaning. Where it ends is another matter. Once the mime knows how to make his body self-sufficient, not dependent upon text or music or scenery, he loses nothing by adding new tools and new accents that can help mold his vision.

The other edge of a mime's limits—and his liberties, for that matter—is at the edge that directly touches his audience. The audience comes to see him; often it pays to come. The mime comes to communicate. Mime, like all art of the theater, makes possible that rather subtle bond between those who watch and those who do. It is a bond based upon trust and a good deal of respect.

Perhaps more than some other theater artists, the mime finds it impossible to perform for himself and be satisfied. The actor has the sound of his voice, something to hear, something to parade in front of even when alone in a room. The dancer has the elation of his physical prowess; the singer has the comfort of his music. But the mime has only the ability to create an illusion for others—it is not an illusion for himself. So Mime is an art that cannot afford to believe it exists and survives simply for the sake of art. It exists for the sake of its audience.

Some mimes forget this. They forget that their primary role is to create a world that communicates itself to an audience.

There are mimes who tend to hide their technique instead of displaying it. They feel that technique is somewhat prosaic, that it is not sufficiently artful. Going beyond technique, there is a good chance that they will lose technique altogether.

Precision goes first; approximation goes next. Soon little of the technique remains. The illusion becomes vague and powerless. And the audience is mystified. Something is happening, but the audience has no clear notion of what and where.

The mime must not forget his ability to communicate, for it is his ability to communicate non-verbally that has attracted and developed his audiences. The contemporary audience is ready to accept the non-verbal skills of the mime because these very skills are what make the mime so appealing. There is an uneasiness with language.

A CHARACTER IN A BECKETT PLAY remarked to her husband, "My dear, have you ever thought we speak a dead language?" Many who are attracted to Mime feel the same way. For some reason, to many of us language does indeed seem dead. It appears to be nothing more than a series of lifeless objects strung together in a hopeless attempt to convey meaning and feeling. Perhaps this has come about because of the disparity between what is said and what is done, because of the weight of bureaucratic pronouncements upon our imagination.

Whatever the reason, the

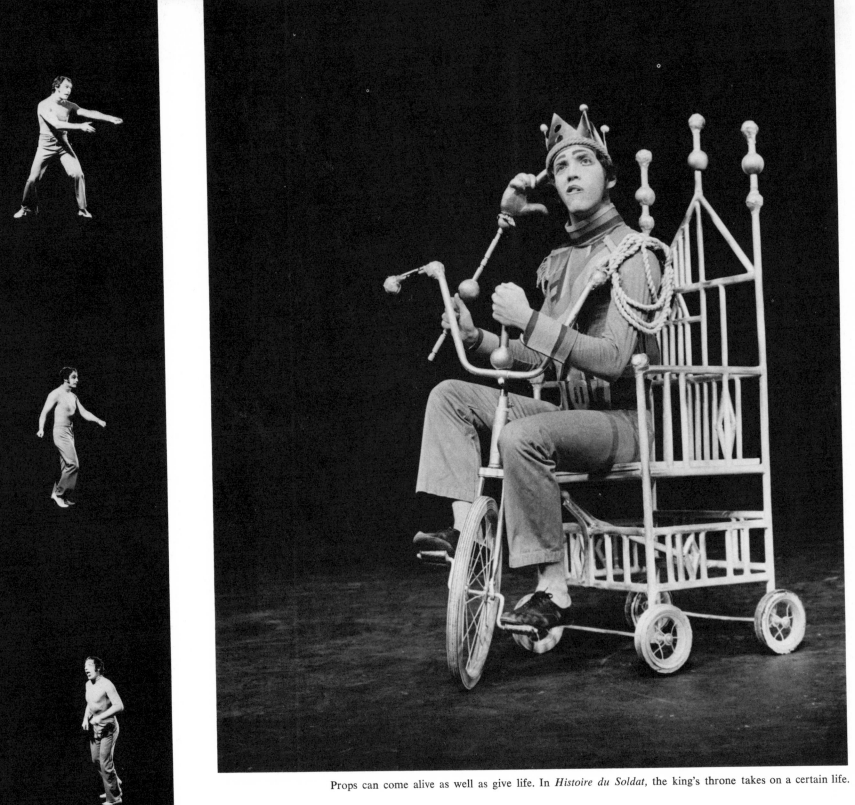

Props can come alive as well as give life. In *Histoire du Soldat*, the king's throne takes on a certain life.

In *Eve and The Serpent,* the tree separates hand from body, thus making two characters.

Sets can be created to emphasize function or they can be used to develop mood. In *Renard*, the set provides multiple levels to perform on.

206

In *L'Histoire du Soldat*, the set is primarily a backdrop before which emotions may be screened.

207

sense of language's inadequacy has been a long time coming. The first tremors could be felt early in the twentieth century in the Dada movement, in Surrealism, in the poetic experiments of Pound and Eliot. On stage, there were Jarry and Pirandello and later Ionesco and Beckett. (Beckett found the language so futile that for a time he created drama without words.) Not surprisingly, as most of this original requestioning of language and its value was taking place, Mime was being rediscovered and remade.

In 1921, a group of actors under the leadership of Jacques Copeau formed a company and school called Le Vieux-Colombier. Copeau wished to renew the actor's position on stage, to make the actor's body as expressive an instrument as his voice. Much was tried. The school at Le Vieux-Colombier masked the face in order to re-emphasize the rest of the body; it re-explored the use of gestures to project meaning. What Le Vieux-Colombier did was not yet Mime, but it was very close. Copeau

This transposition is not a distortion. Poetry is not caricature.

In the mysterious silence of life, each object shows itself as a fantastic being: a fascinating Presence. The subjective reactions which arise in us before this Presence are astounding.

Jean-Louis Barrault, "The Tragic Mime"
in *The Mime* by Jean Dorcy

In the inventiveness of the actor-mime and in his expression is revealed the comic and tragic depth of his Art; this inventiveness is itself linked to the knowledge of life or, in other words, to the observation of man among his fellow-men.

When the actor-mime sustains his dramatic action with the inspiration of his thought, the sensitive response he induces is the echo of his soul, and the gesture becomes a silent inner song. The actor-mime vibrates like the strings of a harp. He is *lyrical: his gesture seems to be invested with a poetic halo.*

Marcel Marceau, "The Poetic Halo"
in *The Mime*

and the rest still saw themselves as actors and not as mimes. (For an informative discussion of the importance of Le Vieux-Colombier upon Mime and, for that matter, a rewarding consideration of Mime itself, read Jean Dorcy's book *The Mime*.)

There are three who make Mime what it is today: Etienne Decroux, Jean-Louis Barrault, and Marcel Marceau. Decroux, a student at Le Vieux-Colombier, is the first rhetorician and theorist of Mime. He claims that Mime was all there at Le Vieux-Colombier, only waiting to be seen on its own. "I invented only to believe in it." With that, he founded the basis for a new Mime grammar.

Barrault and Decroux worked together; with this collaboration, one can say that Mime truly began. Barrault is, without doubt, one of the first men of French theater; a great mime, a great actor, and a great director, he has kept alive a creative intercourse between the art of Mime and the art of acting. Those who have seen *Children of Paradise* will remember Barrault playing

209

the role of Gaspard Deburau, the great Pierrot of the nineteenth century. Decroux played the role of Deburau's father. For all of its other virtues, *Children of Paradise* is a very important film for present Mime. In it, Barrault and Decroux recapture the flavor of an earlier Mime while establishing Mime's claims to a contemporary audience.

Marceau, a student of Decroux, made Mime into an international art with an international audience. His particular style and his subtle skills capture the imagination of those who see him. Marceau has the great performer's ability to make his audience into advocates and students of Mime simply by performing in front of them. The interest in Mime that Marceau has stimulated has helped to develop an entire new generation of professional mimes.

One feels the echoes of Mime throughout contemporary theater—if not true echoes drawn directly from Mime's theory, at least echoes from the spirit of Mime. From Genet's *The Bal-cony* to Peter Brook's production of *Marat/Sade,* from Jarry's *Ubu Roi* to the Marx Brothers' *Night at the Opera,* the non-verbal and the physical have been experimented with and played with. Slowly we have witnessed the rediscovery of their power, giving new and exciting aspects to the shape of human feeling.

More than forty years ago Decroux argued for a theater based upon the art of acting, a theater in which plays were rehearsed before they were written, a theater in which the text was made subordinate to the actor's creative skills.

Now one thinks of the work done by Grotowsky in his Laboratory Theater, where these very principles are being applied. Or one thinks of the work done by Malina and Beck in the Living Theater, or by Chaikin at the Open Theater. Mime has been at least one force to remind the actor of his potential, showing the way to a true collaboration with both the director and the playwright.

Mime has given directly of its techniques and its emphases to other arts. Both theater and dance increasingly employ the freeze, the slow motion, and any number of isolations that spring from Mime. In particular, what Mime has been able to show the other arts is a way to re-create a human reality that is silent but specific.

What, then, does Mime offer to its contemporary audience? It offers a return to the physical— to the gesture made self-sufficient. But Mime does not promote the physical for its own sake or for the sake of visual effects or choreography. Mime's physicality always struggles to project a state of being, of feeling, of meaning. It is an articulate language, in part returning to the mysteries of the ritual, in part remaining in the world of the human. It is in the world before language and before the word, in the beginning of things. However, it reminds one of the power of language and the need for it. The irony of Mime is: if there were no spoken language, it would remind us to create one.

A mimed caress heightens the erotic quality of a sequence. The mimes do not touch, yet the illusion of contact is made. *The Miraculous Mandarin.*

211

Appendices

Episodes and Comments from the History of Mime

Herodotus tells the following story of a mime's attempt to use his art to win fame and fortune. Clisthenes, tyrant of Sicyon in the sixth century B.C., had a beautiful daughter with a handsome dowry and many suitors. He staged a competition of music and poetry to determine who would be her husband. One of the contestants, Hippoclydus, "ordered the flutes to play *Emmeleia,* a tragic dance, and executed this dance with as much grace as ability. His expressive gestures were admired by all. But, not content with this triumph, Hippoclydus had a table brought on which he stood on his head, and, lifting his feet in the air, he executed the same pantomime in this position, gesticulating with his legs as well as he had with his hands." According to history, despite his double triumph, Hippoclydus failed to win the princess.

Athenaeus writes that the Greek mime Telesis, a contemporary of Aeschylus, was so talented that he was able to perform in pantomime the entire Theban War, or, more exactly,

Aeschylus' version of it, *The Seven Against Thebes,* without omitting any events and without any obscurity of meaning.

Pylades was perhaps the most famous Roman mime; he competed with all about him, just as they competed with him. Macrobius relates the following story: "Hilas, disciple and competitor of Pylades, once executed a monologue ending with the words 'the great Agamemnon.' Hilas to express them made all the gestures of a man that wants to measure another bigger than himself. Then Pylades, who was in the pit, unable to contain himself, cried out, 'Friend, by this you make Agamemnon only a *big* man, not a great man.' On this the people immediately called out for Pylades to perform it himself; he complied; and when he came to that part for which he had publicly censured his disciple, he represented by his gestures, and attitudes, the countenance of a person immersed in deep meditation, pointing out, very properly by his action, that a man greater than others was he who had pro-

founder thoughts." Among other things, this passage shows that Roman Mime was still rooted to the words of a specific text, the mime's function being to paraphrase it in a non-verbal language.

Pylades was the great tragic mime of Rome; Bathyllus, his contemporary, was the great comic mime. Both were forces in the state and did not fear to antagonize the Emperor Augustus. In fact, they were sometimes useful political diversions, distracting the public from affairs of state. Augustus once complained of their constant bickering and competitiveness, but was reminded of their political value by Pylades, who remarked: "Caesar, it is in your interest to have the people involved in our disputes; this prevents them from paying attention to your deeds."

Four hundred years after Pylades and Bathyllus, Cassiodorus presents a quite accurate picture of Roman Mime, especially the mime's continuing reliance upon an established text. "The actor appears on stage amidst the ac-

215

clamations of the spectators. A chorus of instruments accompanies him. With only hand movements he explains to the eyes the poem that is being sung by the musicians, and, using composed gestures, as in writing one uses letters, he speaks to the eye, renders the slightest nuance of the discourse, and demonstrates, without talking, all that writing could express. The same body shows us Hercules or Venus, a king or a soldier, a man or a woman, an old man or an adolescent, and the illusion is so great that you think you are seeing several in one, such are the variations of the actor in his posture, walks and gestures."

England produced a great mime in the eighteenth century, John Rich, whose stage name was Lun. Rich started to perform at a time when English theater was being influenced to a high degree by Italian *commedia dell'arte* and French harlequinade. Illiterate and awkward in his diction, Rich was forced to act in silence. This turned out to be his virtue. He transformed the classic harlequinade into a totally non-verbal show and thus exposed the potential of Mime to assert itself amidst the clutter of stage machinery, sets, costumes, songs, and music. David Garrick, a theatrical competitor and himself an important actor of the period, wrote of him:

When Lun appeared with faultless
   art and whim
He gave the power of speech to
   every limb.
Though masked and mute, conveyed his quick intent
And told in frolic gestures all he
   meant. . . .

Nineteenth-century France produced two important mimes: Gaspard Deburau and Louis Rouffe. Deburau, who crystallized the character of Pierrot, attracted much of Paris to his Funambules. Rouffe, performing primarily in Marseilles, remains a lesser-known figure, although there is evidence to indicate that his contribution to the art of Mime may have been greater than is commonly understood. In this light, Charles Hacks, a nineteenth-century commentator and historian of Mime and gesture, presents us with an intriguing comparison of Deburau and Rouffe. "Deburau grimaces, expresses, jumps, whirls, contorts but does not talk; to the clowning *Pierrot,* he did not know how to, or *did not want to,* add the *mime*; therefore from him nothing has survived but his Pierrot. Yet, with one more step, he would have escaped saltation, dance and 'funambulie' and would have created the complete work as the genius of Rouffe did after him. . . . Louis Rouffe appears, illiterate like Deburau, but, one must add, more refined and more intelligent. He is to reconsider the entire art and, in a thirty-three-year career, he stages and reconstitutes saltation, antique Mime, the whole history of gesture, and definitively establishes pantomime, giving it for a base the art of miming."

Historical References:

Broadbent, R. J. *A History of Pantomime*. London: Simpkin, Marshall, Hamilton, and Kent, 1902. (Reissued in paperback, New York: Citadel Press, 1965.)

Elyot, Thomas. *The Boke Named the Governour*. London, 1531. (Available in various contemporary editions.)

Hacks, Charles. *Le Geste*. Paris: Librairie Marpon and Flammarion, 1892.

Lucian. *Collected Works*. Tr. and ed. H. W. Fowler and F. G. Fowler. Oxford, 1905.

Niklaus, Thelma. *Harlequin*. New York: George Braziller, 1956.

Weaver, John. *A History of Mimes and Pantomimes*. London, 1728.

Short Discussion of Flip Sequences

There are six sequences of flips. Three of them (The Pull, The Weight Lifter, and The Walk) start on page 5, moving from the front of the book to the back. The other three (The Tow, The Cyclist, and The Run) start on page 214, moving from the back of the book forward. With some practice, you will be able to integrate the top and bottom, forward and backward sequences to make a continuous flow of action. Thus The Pull will move into The Tow, from pulling to being pulled. Similarly The Walk will become The Run.

The Pull and The Tow: Taken together, these two form a tug-of-war sequence; at some point, the mime becomes two characters pulling himself and being pulled. Besides the development of the character in the fight, the main points illustrated by these two sequences are clic, resistance, compensation, manipulation, re-actions, and slides. Notice the effect of surprise on the reaction.

The Weight Lifter: The bravado of the weight lifter is challenged by the mass he has to lift. The main points illustrated by this sequence are manipulation, particularly the approach and the grab; clic, crucial in the first unsuccessful attempt to lift; resistance; and, of course, the bend as he is crushed under the weight.

The Cyclist: This sequence combines the profile walk with the bicycle, which is a variation of the profile run.

The Walk and The Run: In these two sequences, the character recognizes someone at a distance. Not being recognized in turn, he quickens his pace in order to catch up. The main points illustrated by this sequence are pressure walk, pressure run, focus at a distance, tendency, and positive pressure.

Glossary

[Italicized words appear as entries elsewhere in the glossary.]

Approach, 84. The first step in manipulation. Motions preceding the grab or *take* of an object.

Attitude, 147–149. A physical position that expresses a psychological state.

Behavior, 149. The conduct of a character reflected by his movements and positions.

Center, the, 24–25. The point in the body where energy and movement begin. For example, the torso is the center for the whole body; the palm, the center for the hand.

Center, to, 161–162. To place oneself well on stage in order to take advantage of the available space during the performance of a *pantomime.*

Chased Foot, 116. In an illusory *walk* or run, the foot that is "blown away" by the *stepping foot.*

Clic, 73–74. One of the three elements of a movement. (The other two elements are *pressure* and *immobility.*) A short outburst of energy that marks the beginning and end of a movement. In French, sometimes called "the toc," although "toc" does not necessarily imply an outburst of energy.

Compensation, 90–93. The double motion of the body that allows the *mime* to mark a fixed point in space.

Conflict, 166–167. The contradictions that dramatize a *situation.*

Drop, 127. The action of the foot in stepping down from a raised position.

Ecology of Mime, 183. Application of the *Law of Economy;* the avoidance of wasted motions and actions.

Economy, Law of, 180–183. Doing the most with the least. This is the backbone of the art of *Mime.*

Event, 158–159. The smallest particle of comprehensible movement.

Fidelity, Principle of, 85, 89, 160. The need to remember the positioning of an imaginary object and the ability to return to it. It also entails honoring the planes and dimensions of an imaginary object.

Flip, 82. The swift change of direction of a segment of the body.

Forms of Mime Representation, 184–193. The shapes and structures that a *pantomime* may take. Among them: anecdotal or narrative; symbolic or metaphoric; satirical; figurative or animation; abstract; surrealistic; realistic or fantastic.

Freeze, 72. An instant of *immobility* during an action.

Immobility, 68, 71. One of the three elements of a movement. (The other two elements are *clic* and *pressure.*) Immobility prepares or concludes a movement.

Improvisation (Games), 171–176. Technique of games that the *mime* uses to discover and create *situa-*

tions and characters. Examples: Pick Up and Follow; Pick Up and Twist; and What-When-Where.

Isolation, 11, 42. The technique of moving each segment of the body independently.

Land, 126. Used in the step up, it is the dual action of the legs to create the illusion of reaching a new step.

Level, 127. The raised position from which the body steps down.

Lift, 126. The action of raising the body in stepping up.

Manipulation, 83–86. The technique of handling imaginary objects, consisting of *approach, take,* and *release.*

Mark, 126. Used in the step up, it is the action to indicate a new level.

Mime, 4–7. The art of creating the illusion of reality by the movements and positions of the human body. It is the art of imagining the world together with an audience. When the word is not capitalized, the performer is a mime.

Mimetic Imitation, 17. The ability to adapt the body to the properties of things it is dealing with. Example: imitation of a butterfly by the fluttering movement of the hand. In French, "mimetisme."

Mimodrama, 175–176. A *pantomime* presenting dramatic relationships between several *mimes.*

Necessity, sense of, 164. The *mime's* ability to determine the minimum time, space, or movement required to convey meaning. Compare with *sufficiency.*

Odyssey Complex, 171. The temptation of a novice to do everything he can think of on a given subject.

Pan, 117. Action by which a *mime* creates a panoramic effect when he uses a sideways *pressure walk.*

Pantomime, 155. A composition in *Mime* that stands by itself. Sometimes used synonomously with Mime (or the mime), especially in antique Mime.

Pressure, 69–70. One of the three elements of a movement. (The other two elements are *clic* and *immobility.*) Pressure is the force that maintains a position or sustains a movement. Also in a *pressure walk* or run, pressure is the action of one foot as it pushes its heel down, *chasing* away the other foot, page 116.

Pressure Walk, 116–118. An illusory *walk* in place in which one foot seems to be pushed away by the action of the other. Compare with the *profile,* or *vacuum, walk.* The pressure run is the companion to the pressure walk, page 121.

Priority, to give, 175. The ability of a *mime* to make room for the initiatives of a fellow mime when both are performing together.

Profile Walk, 119–120. An illusory *walk* in place, also called the *vacuum* walk, in which one foot seems to be pulled by the action of the other. Compare with the *pressure walk.* The profile run is the companion to the profile walk, page 122.

Projection, power of, 42. The ability to reach out to an audience. The *mime* projects both his inner and outer worlds.

Release, 86. In *manipulation,* the moment when the *mime* opens his hands and leaves the object.

Resistance, 80. In *Mime,* a synonym for weight. An object's property of resisting an outside force.

Saltation, 108. An archaic term for acrobatic dance.

Silence, 163. A dimension that a *mime* works in, similar to the dimensions of space and time. It is essential even when broken.

Situation, 160–164. An *event,* or group of events, specifically defined in space and time.

Slow Motion, 61. Important aspect of *Mime* technique that stresses the ability to execute a movement slowly and continuously. The French mime Etienne Decroux

calls it "le Fondu"; in dance it is called "the adagio."

Stepping foot, 116. In a *walk* or a run, the foot that starts the action.

Sufficiency, sense of, 164. The mime's ability to stretch an action without losing or distorting its meaning.

Tableau, 172. Usually a frozen position held at the beginning or at the end of a piece.

Take, 85. In *manipulation,* the moment when the *mime* defines the shape of an object. It consists of touch and close. Commonly called "the grab."

Tempo, 163. The speed and rhythm at which an action is executed.

Tendency, 139, 145. The tilt of the body in a specific direction.

Tension, 72, 139, 147. The accumulation of energy and *pressure* in the body just prior to movement.

Timing, 163. The time relation between two successive actions. The relative duration of each act or movement in a succession of ac-

tions or movements.

Vacuum, 119. In the *profile walk* or run, the action of one foot as it raises its heel, "pulling" in the other foot.

Walk, 113–121. There are two walks, the *pressure walk* and the *profile walk,* also called the *vacuum* walk. Traditionally, mimes have not distinguished between these walks. Usually the walk is simply called "the walk in place" or "the walk on the spot," expressions that cover any illusory walk.

Wave, 54. The technique of undulation of the body or part of it.

Whip Effect, 109. Undulation of the body in reaction to a push or pull.

Zero: Disposition, 141; Position, 11; Pressure, 141–142. A neutral position or state, used as a point of reference.

Zoom Effect, 117. Zoom-in and zoom-out effects are created by the special use of the *pressure walk* toward or away from the audience.

Credits: Performances and Photographs

The Claude Kipnis Mime Theatre has been in existence for over a decade. It has performed in France, Belgium, Holland, Norway, Finland, Israel, and the United States. Its size has varied from three to eight performers. The pantomimes of the present repertoire were all conceived and staged by Claude Kipnis. The following listing presents some of the major pieces in the repertoire, some historical information, and credits. The photographs used in this book have been listed under the appropriate production.

Men and Dreams. Premiered in 1962, Tel Aviv, Israel. Sets by Amiram Shamir. Music especially composed by Noam Sheriff. This is a series of short pantomimes, some of which are "The Bottle," "Main Street," "The Life Guard," "The Bus Ride," "The Village," "Eve and The Serpent," "The Young Hood," and "The Cabinet Minister." (Solo photographs of Kipnis are from the original production and were provided by Theatre Diocan, Tel Aviv. The two group photographs of The Balladins with Kipnis, Rudy Benda, and Dina Kipnis are from a later production and are courtesy of Eugene Tellez.)

Fiddler in the *shtetle,* page 76
Young Hood, page 153.
The Teacher, page 182.
The Cabinet Minister, page 188.
Eve and The Serpent, page 205.
The Balladins, pages 177 and 178.

The Miraculous Mandarin. Premiered in 1967, Boston, Massachusetts. Commissioned by the Boston Opera Company. Music by Bela Bartok. Sets and costumes by Dina Kipnis. This pantomime was adapted from a scenario by Melchior Lengyel.

Thugs (Bob Griffard, Mike Hoit, Doug Day), page 32.
Mandarin and Girl (Kipnis and Chris Swing), page 43.
Young man and Girl (Kipnis and Swing), page 44.
Old man and Girl (Kipnis, Hoit, and Swing), page 45.
Young Man Freezes (Griffard and Kipnis), page 71.
A Mimed Caress (Griffard and Swing), page 210.

Opus Blue . . . Is Pink. Premiered in 1969, Urbana, Illinois. Commissioned by the University of Illinois. Sets and costumes by Dina Kipnis. This is a series of contemporary pantomime pieces with especially composed music.

"The Crowd." Music by Ben Johnston. Masks by Frank Gallo.

Crowd Collapsing (Day, Donna Gibbons, Benda, Hoit, Swing, Griffard, Rita Nachtmann, and Navvab Fisher), page 186.

"Point of View." Music by Edwin London.

The Statue (Nachtmann, Day, Benda), page 187.

"Au Clair de la Lune." Music by Neely Bruce.

The Astronauts (Griffard and Benda), page 200.

The Pierrots (Kipnis, Fisher, Gail Maxwell, Debbie Langerman, and Day), page 201.

"The Party."

The Waiter (Kipnis), page 49.

Histoire du Soldat and **Renard.** Premiered together in 1970, Urbana, Illinois. Commissioned by the Krannert Center of the Performing Arts at the University of Illinois. (By special invitation performed at the Stravinsky Celebration under the auspices of the Boston Opera Company, Boston, Massachusetts, in 1972.) Music by Igor Stravinsky. Sets, costumes and masks by Dina Kipnis. *Histoire* has narration and dialogue; the text is by Ramuz. In *Renard,* the musical score includes singers.

Histoire du Soldat

Devil Drinking (Kipnis), page 87.

The Card Game (Day and Kipnis), page 198.

The King (Hoit), page 204.

The Party (Marty Sausser, Griffard, Hoit, Gibbons and Day), page 207.

Renard

Mother Fox (Kipnis), page 152.

Animal Chorus (Kipnis, Sausser, Day, Gibbons, Nachtmann, and Hoit), page 179.

Goat and Cat (Hoit and Nachtmann), page 190.

Animal Argument (*top:* Sausser and Gibbons; *bottom:* Hoit, Kipnis, Nachtmann and Day), page 206.

The Legend of the Stonecutter. Premiered in 1972, Provincetown Playhouse, New York City. Masks by Amiram Shamir. This is a pantomime with narration for children.

The Sun (Kipnis), page 192.

Other pantomimes performed by the Kipnis Mime Theatre are Dukas' *The Sorcerer's Apprentice,* Kabalevsky's *The Comedians,* Stravinsky's *Suite No. 2,* and Mussorgsky's *Pictures at an Exhibition.*